Jumpstart Your _______, Vol V

11 Inspiring Entrepreneurs Share Stories and Strategies on How to Jumpstart Many Areas of Your Life, Business, Relationships, and Health

Compiled by Katrina Sawa

CEO & Founder of JumpstartYourBizNow.com, JumpstartPublishing.net and 12x Int'l Best-Selling Author

Jumpstart
PUBLISHING

Get to Know the 11 Inspiring Authors in this Book!

There's ONE page online where you can access all the authors' websites and special offers from this book to make it super easy for you to follow up and connect with them further.

Go to www.JumpstartBookAuthors.com right now before you forget. For a list of authors and their chapters, turn to the Table of Contents page.

Katrina Sawa, Speaker, 12x Int'l Best-Selling Author, Publisher, Award-Winning Business & Marketing Coach to Entrepreneurs Who Want More LOVE in Their Lives and MONEY in Their Businesses!

Published by K. Sawa Marketing International Inc. A.K.A. Jumpstart Publishing. P.O. Box 6, Roseville, CA 95661. (916) 872-4000 www.JumpstartPublishing.net

DISCLAIMER AND/OR LEGAL NOTICES

While all attempts have been made to verify information provided in this book and its ancillary materials, neither the authors nor publisher assume any responsibility for errors, inaccuracies, or omissions and are not responsible for any financial loss by customer in any manner. Any slights of people or organizations are unintentional. If advice concerning legal, financial, accounting, health or related matters is needed, the services of a qualified professional should be sought. This book and its associated ancillary materials, including verbal and written training, are not intended for use as a source of legal, financial or accounting advice.

EARNINGS & INCOME DISCLAIMER

With respect to the reliability, accuracy, timeliness, usefulness, adequacy, completeness, and/or suitability of information provided in this book, Katrina Sawa, K. Sawa Marketing International Inc., its partners, associates, affiliates, consultants, and/or presenters make no warranties, guarantees, representations, or claims of any kind. Readers' results will vary. This book and all products and services are for educational and informational purposes only. Katrina Sawa and/or K. Sawa Marketing International Inc. is not responsible for the success or failure of your business, personal, health or financial decisions relating to any information presented by Katrina Sawa, K. Sawa Marketing International Inc., or company products/services.

Any examples, stories, reference, or case studies are for illustrative purposes only and should not be interpreted as testimonies and/or examples of what readers and/or consumers can generally expect from the information.

ISBN: 978-1-7358666-4-2

PRINTED IN THE UNITED STATES OF AMERICA

Dedication

This book is dedicated to Entrepreneurs everywhere who have the desire and mission to make a bigger impact with those they serve.

Here's to creating and enjoying the business and life of your dreams!

Special thank you to my husband Jason and step-daughter Riley who support me 100% on all of my entrepreneurial endeavors. And thank you to all of the awesome jumpstart authors that have written their stories and strategies in this and previous books.

Praise for the *Jumpstart Your _____* Books

These are my favorite books to read.

"This is the perfect time for this book to come out. I'm so glad I bought this! So many incredible stories of ways to jumpstart your business, your love life, your dreams, anything you can think of. These are my favorite books to read. I definitely recommend this book!" - Candi & Sean Douglas

Great read -- Short doses of inspiration

"This is a great book. Many tidbits of motivation. You can read any chapter and gain inspiration to take on the day's challenges. I love the stories and perspectives provided." - Karen T. Peak

Another great book by Katrina Sawa & Friends

"Katrina Sawa always brings her readers beneficial info for growing a business in the current marketplace." - PK Odle

Excellent Co-Authors with a variety of backgrounds

"Really great content, the authors here have a variety of backgrounds which is great for insight!" - Matt Brauning

A Great Source of Inspiration!

"Being an Entrepreneur is a really tough... but rewarding job! Sometimes you need a little extra encouragement to push you through the rough times. This is an incredible book, packed with all kinds of inspiring entrepreneur stories. I found nuggets of wisdom and inspiration all at the same time!" - Richard B. Greene

Katrina Sawa Never Disappoints

"Katrina Sawa never disappoints when she is delivering information to her audience of fans and she certainly delivers with her latest book. Thank you, Katrina, for gathering this group of experts to provide us with a great resource." - RL Escobar-Balcom

There is something for Everyone!

"Jumpstart Your _____ is filled with powerful stories and insightful takeaways that can help you grow your business and more importantly, enjoy your life. There is something for everyone! Bottom line - this book ROCKS!" - Craig Duswalt, Keynote Speaker, Author, Podcaster, and Creator of the brands RockStar Marketing and Rock Your Life.

So much great Inspiration!

"Hard to believe so much great information is available in ONE book. Whatever you dream... you can achieve! You are bound to find something impactful in this book!" - Marguerite Crespillo

Entrepreneurship isn't easy but it is worth it and these ladies show you why.

"This is a must-read if you are looking for inspiration, realistic strategies or just a reason not to give up. These women and the stories of what they have done in their businesses can give you that. So glad that I made this book purchase. Thanks, ladies for putting this collection of stories together." – Samantha M.

Inspiring and Motivating Book

"Each author wrote of relevant information. Every woman I know could benefit from reading this book. I truly enjoyed reading this." - Melanie

This book should be accompanied by a glass of wine!

"Katrina has put together authors that have written short vignettes that are like micro-guides to getting your life or business on track." – Jason Ciment, Author of the book "I Need More Clients"

Great book with lots of info!

"Wonderfully compiled book for every part of life!" – Amber Trail

A must-read!

"This book has many inspiring stories that can help you jumpstart your personal life or your business. A fantastic tool to have by your bed-side table!" – Sandra D. Pablos

This book has great tips to Jumpstart your Life—your health—and your Wealth!

"I really enjoyed this book! Short, impactful chapters with quick, actionable tips and suggestions regarding your life, health, wellness, wealth, and business. I especially was intrigued by the "Jumpstart your Weight Loss" section by Tonya Rios where she mentions EFT (Emotional Freedom Technique)--better known as Tapping. I'm going to have to check that out because it sounds really interesting. Whatever you want to "Jumpstart" in your life--this book can help you do it!" – Donald E. Franceschi

TABLE OF CONTENTS

This book is divided first by topics relating to jumpstarting one's life and self, then by business-oriented chapters. Within each section, chapters are categorized alphabetically.

Introduction

This book, *Jumpstart Your _____, Volume V*, is for you if you need a jumpstart in any area of your life, career, business, mindset, health, relationships, prosperity, beliefs, and more!

This is the fifth book in the *Jumpstart Your* _____ series, and we keep getting new, fresh topics, content, and authors! This volume has 10 new authors in addition to myself. We have a wide variety of chapters, with advice for the business owner, woman, man, professional, online marketer, as well as the person who wants to improve his or her life, career, health, and even relationship with themselves and/or significant other. It's fun to see who comes through with each book, and what expertise they bring.

The authors with whom I have collaborated on this book are experts in their industries and in what they teach. Our goal is to provide a book that shows you how and why you should consider jumpstarting many of the areas covered within these chapters.

If you enjoy any one or more of the stories and chapters within this book, please reach out and contact the author(s). They want to know that their chapter encouraged you, inspired you, or motivated you in some way. They also want to know how they can help you. Each author has provided some kind of next step or free gift at the end of their chapter, to give you the opportunity to learn more. Don't stop with this book: please take the initiative and reach out for more information, more help, and more advice for whatever you might be trying to jumpstart in your life right now. Who knows maybe after your initial read-through of this book, you will pick it up a couple years from now and decide to jumpstart something else!

This edition of *Jumpstart Your* _____ can help literally anyone, I believe. There are chapters you'll find immediately helpful, and some you may not need until years from now--but keep it handy just in case, because you never know!

Half of the chapters in this book will help you jumpstart an area of your personal life, and half of them are geared more towards helping business owners. Whether or not you have a business, one day you may! Order extra copies of these books for friends, family, or clients; they will appreciate your thoughtfulness.

What about you? Do you have an area of expertise about which you could write in one of our Jumpstart Your _____ books? One thing I know to be true is that most entrepreneurs really do need a book in this day and age. You need to be an author to really be seen as the expert in your industry, or even in the company for which you work. Writing a whole book by yourself is a lot of work, takes a lot of time, and sometimes costs a lot of money. Being an author in a compilation book like this one, however, is a lot less cumbersome, less stressful, and less costly. It's also helpful when somebody puts it all together for you, and you don't have to worry about all the details of editing, cover design, proofing, and publishing. (That's what we do here at Jumpstart Publishing.)

I've been in business since 2002. I've been an author in now 17 compilation books, plus three of my own full-length books. I have put together this opportunity to become a published author, with very little effort and work on your part--if you're interested. Contact me if you might be interested in being an author in the next *Jumpstart Your* _____ book, and share your story! Go to www.JumpstartPublishing.net for details.

And if you've ever thought about starting, growing, or marketing your own business, and/or becoming an author or speaker, please reach out to me; I'm extremely passionate about helping anybody build a profitable business doing what they love. - Katrina Sawa

Jumpstart
Your Life/Self
Chapters

Jumpstart Your Career

5 Steps to Land Your Dream Job or Build Your Dream Team

By Shawna Champlin

If you've ever read the word "career" and mumbled to yourself, "This doesn't apply to me; I'm a business owner!" then I encourage you to read on, and you'll see how this word actually applies to most people. Read on, because whether you own a business or want to stay in the corporate lane, I'm going to share some tips for *Landing Your Dream Job* or *Building Your Dream Team*, regardless of which lane you are in.

I'll give you a little backstory before I share more. Some people know from an early age what job they want to do for a living, while others know they never want to work for anyone else but themselves. Then there are people like me, who start in the job market, then realize they actually want to be self-employed.

Over my 30-year career in Corporate America, I served in major for-profit and non-profit industries. I worked my way from the bottom, earning promotions into various roles, and led several teams. I leaped into management, promoted many employees, and worked with countless leaders and C-Suites. Working 70- to sometimes over 100-hour workweeks became my norm. It was not unheard of to work four days straight around the clock. Within a 3-year period, I was hospitalized 3 times, almost died, and frequently took antibiotics. I made my j-o-b the priority instead of me. I finally asked myself, "Is this healthy?" Once I came to realize I was an unhealthy and unhappy workaholic, I decided I was done working for someone else. It was time to focus on my own mission.

As a single mother, I was scared to become an entrepreneur. While maintaining my crazy work schedule, I dipped my toes into a networking side hustle and then ventured to start a small business. But I kept getting pulled back into the demands (and bigger, more consistent income) of my corporate job, so I finally scrapped both ventures. Eventually, I married the love of my life and finished financially helping my son through college.

I was accustomed to the certainty my job provided, even if I was fed-up with the job itself. But I had to admit that my corporate job duties did not fully utilize my strengths. I could quickly identify skill sets of employees and co-workers, get anyone to perform, and easily motivate resources. For a couple of years, I had hired a business coach to show me what to do to build a business on the side, but honestly, I didn't believe it was possible or that I could actually do it. I finally realized I had the career trajectory "secret sauce," and I had to muster the courage to move forward.

Then I thought, "I'm going to be 51 in a month." I began to question myself.

Do I really want this anymore?

Is this how I want to continue to work and live?

Am I living my dream?

Isn't there a better way?

My honest answers were my catalyst; I finally heard my inner pleas for help. I had experienced many health setbacks and my body, mind, and spirit had suffered enough. I paid off all my bills, hopped onto my husband's benefits, and submitted my resignation. On my 51st birthday, I celebrated my freedom and began building what is now my dream job—my business as an Interview, Career, and Life Coach, called Shining Outcomes LLC. I took the long way around in my career, kicking and screaming the entire way to becoming a business owner, until I finally jumped in to live my dreams.

Our careers make up so much of the time we spend on this planet, so we better enjoy them. To waste energy on a company where you are miserable, to work in a culture or an environment that goes against your values, to put off building your own business because of fear—those actions are futile. You are more deserving than that! Whether you own a business or are in a job, ask yourself: is it the perfect situation for you? If it's not, we need to explore what that perfect situation could look like. It's imperative to know what you want from this life, and that requires asking yourself some hard questions:

> *What are your long-term goals, mission, and purpose?*
>
> *What is your desired lifestyle, and does your career align with it?*

I'm writing about jumpstarting your career because I can't wait to help you land the job you want, build and empower your dream team, and level up your career as the leader this world needs.

The number one obstacle with which clients need help in my coaching business is finding "the words." The words you use can make or break how you sell yourself and what you bring to the table. Often, the most qualified person at the table is the quietest. You may have the skills or experience and believe you can do the job, but you may not know how to express these vital details. This skill goes beyond an interview. Whether it's through a resume, a thank-you letter, a verbal reference, a letter of recommendation, a meeting with a team/boss/client, a self-review, an employee review, a performance improvement plan, a job posting, procedure development, a business presentation, a client contract, and so on, knowing the importance of words—their meanings, descriptors, and intentions—is an integral and necessary skill for capturing content and speaking succinctly and eloquently.

When an opportunity presents itself, you have to jump on it and use your words in a compelling way, or the opportunity will pass you by. Speaking (and word choice) in each of the aforementioned scenarios involves the art of "selling." Every one of those scenarios is an opportunity to influence outcomes. You have this capability—you just might need some guidance and practice to hone your "wording" skills and generate the results you want. This works whether you're trying to land the job, hire the right people, move into leadership, etc., because how you do anything is how you do everything.

Words are really significant. Let me give you a couple of examples.

A client who was a Business Analyst came to me with "gathered requirements, completed testing, and assisted with user-acceptance testing" listed as previous job responsibilities on their resume. However, they hadn't included their additional duties of backlog maintenance, issue management, disaster recovery support, integration testing, bug-fix testing, implementation, and post-implementation support monitoring—all of which the client regularly performed, and all of which were key word search items in the job posting. This client landed the job after incorporating our edits.

Another client didn't believe their skills qualified them for a leadership role, as their title didn't state "Management." I pointed out that this client regularly mentored new sales members, developed and negotiated large sales contracts, and consistently penetrated and expanded their sales market. With a little time and work together, this client landed a Director job at another company.

Preparing the right words and using those words strategically is critical to your success—and you can do it without sounding arrogant, and while building influence and landing the opportunities you deserve.

By Shawna Champlin

5 Steps to Land Your Dream Job or Build Your Dream Team

Before you jumpstart your career, make sure you're in the right career for you—whether you plan on building your own business or working for a company. This means knowing what motivates you, what fulfills you, what supports the life you want to live, and whether you have your own mission or wish to work for another company's mission to support, propagate, and deliver. As a business owner, this means "what's in it for them"—your potential team member—and this becomes the basis for some of your introductory interview questions.

Step 1: Identify Your Skill Sets.

This requires a thorough analysis of all your skills, talents, and experiences, what you can learn to expand this list, and how you will contribute to the growth of an organization by applying your unique skills and talents.

As a business owner, this means establishing what skill sets you'll need from team members and what your business can offer them in terms of potential growth opportunities and expanding their skill sets while perpetuating your business' mission.

Step 2: Line Up Your Documentation.

For a jobseeker, this means polishing up your resume, cover letter, and thank-you letter. Your resume must be results-oriented, not task-oriented, and include the key search words listed within the job posting. Your cover letter and thank-you letter must succinctly address the needs of the company and assert that you are the solution.

As a business owner, your job posting needs to inform jobseekers what you are looking for, and it must also convey why someone would want to work with your company—the benefits are crucial. I had a client whose company observed half-day Fridays and 95% of weekends off, and didn't recognize it was an appealing lifestyle benefit. As soon as we added those company perks to the posting, several qualified candidates applied.

Step 3: Update Your References.

As a jobseeker, you must have strong references. I help clients master the essential trick to utilizing references, which makes them irresistible to hiring managers. Remember, references are essentially recommendations and testimonials; you had better get yours in order before you apply.

As a business owner, you must check references and ask the right questions to verify your candidate's experience, while making sure they fit your company culture, goals, and team dynamic.

Step 4: Practice Your Interview Skills.

I cannot stress enough how practicing your interview with a skilled coach can make a difference. This practice puts you into a situation where having the "words" can influence the overall process. Enhancing your interview skills will boost your confidence and prove that you can represent yourself accurately and articulately.

As a business owner, this practice is imperative on both sides of the fence. The interview is two-sided; you are being interviewed just as much as you are interviewing a candidate. Practicing what you will ask, knowing what responses you are looking for from a potential team member, and accurately representing your company, team dynamic, and work culture are significant factors for your team prospects. To land the right team member for your company, you must sell as well as interview.

Step 5: Put Yourself Out There, Apply, and Follow Up.

Diligence, consistency, and resilience will help you throughout the process. You must track the jobs and companies to which you apply, noting the status of the process. This is where your follow-up and thank-you letter skills move into high gear, and with the right words, the stress eases.

As a business owner, you must learn how to scan resumes, complete interviews, and respond to candidates quickly. Although these tasks might seem administrative, the process requires efficient skill set identification, interview practice, and sales methods in order to land the top candidates for your dream team.

Once you've landed the job or built your dream team, you will continue to grow and acquire more skills; thus, you'll be able to level up and elevate all aspects of your career, including compensation, promotions, bonuses, new projects, leadership of new efforts, etc.

Becoming a new or emerging leader can be overwhelming. That's why you want someone like me to help you throughout your career path: landing the job, promoting, building teams, developing top performers, fostering a business culture, and expanding into leadership—because we are always evolving. I'd love to help you continue to grow and live a life you love while gaining the shining outcomes you deserve. **Please go online and grab the free resources I've put together for you at www.ShiningOutcomes.com/jumpstart.** And here's to creating the life you love!

About the Author

Shawna Champlin

Shawna Champlin is a results-driven Interview, Career, & Life Coach, motivational speaker, and bestselling author. For decades, she has helped jobseekers and business owners alike find their confidence, identify what they bring to the table, improve their self-sales skills, polish their competencies, plan their career trajectories, and more. Shawna helps you strategize your overall career options, dreams, and goals so you can truly live a life you love.

Jumpstart Your Habits

8 Ways to Create Miracles in Your Life

By Rahul Sharma

What habits do you have that are serving you... and not serving you?

Let's take a moment to examine your habits, good and bad, and see if there is room for improvement, shall we?

First, let me share that according to *The American Journal of Psychology*, "Habit, from the standpoint of psychology, is defined as a more or less fixed way of thinking, willing, or feeling acquired through previous repetition of a mental experience."

Shall we take a minute to think about a habit you are currently forming in your life, or perhaps a past habit? Now, ponder over whether you find it exciting. You are either envisioning a better version of yourself, or dreading it. Or perhaps you are considering adopting some new habits into your lifestyle.

Now let us examine an instance where people say one must include greens in their diet each day. Is it really all about the benefits of vegetables? Or is it also about the habit of consciously attempting to live a better and healthier life? We all understand the need to teach good habits, but the question is, are you finally ready to do something about it? After all, it is about taking action, or as my coach Dr. Delatorro "Big Deal" McNeal, says, "Taking Consistent Imperfect Action."

Are you ready to take action and design your own life?

If your answer to the question above was yes, I might be able to help you out. What I bring to the table are some tools that have helped me over the years, tools that are not based on guesswork but on solid wisdom and sound principles. Now, if we may, let's travel back in time, shall we? When I started swimming again for fitness two years ago, I was eager to go back to swimming since I had always loved it as a youngster and growing up. The pool at my gym had a 25-meter lap, and I knew nothing could stop me. However, the first day of getting back into that routine was surprisingly tough. Even one lap felt like a challenge, and I had to take regular breaks before the second and third laps.

And to make matters worse, I was deadbeat by the end of the fourth lap. Something was not adding up. I was out of practice and had forgotten the technique. On my way home, I engaged in my usual mind talk to figure out what had gone wrong. I considered a few options and studied more about swimming to be better equipped next time. I prepared myself through more mind talk and set a goal of eight laps without stopping, which may seem unrealistic now that I am writing it down. But I did it, and I gradually increased the number of laps. In just three weeks, I could swim for 40 laps without stopping. The result was a small instance of success because of the habits I developed over time, and this mindset will help you navigate through more pressing life matters.

Let me introduce you to HABITS4MIRACLES: 8 habits we can incorporate into our daily lives, a tiny bit at a time, to clean our brains and make room for finding solutions.

While I can't say I believe in miracles, I believe in the power of small habits over time to create transformation—the type of transformation that, in many ways, is a miracle.

M — Mind talk

The link between success and failure can come down to positive mind talk. Also known as self-talk, it's remodeling our brains to keep them in "happy mode." Studies show that simply thinking about a positive event can lengthen feelings of joy and reduce worry. Our subconscious brain can't distinguish between what's real and what's imagined. Reliving those experiences in our minds can be just as tangible as when they happened. So, you have full permission to talk to yourself. You can even address yourself by name. Studies have shown people who use their name during the mind talk process rather than 'I' display higher self-confidence and self-esteem. (Maybe avoid doing this out loud at meetings!).

I — Ideation

Through the practice of mind talk, ideas will come. But an idea without execution is, well, nothing. We need to take notes when they come to our minds. The more you write down your thoughts, the more ideas you'll have. And the more you act on your ideas, the more will flow your way. An average human mind thinks about 48 thoughts in a single minute. Ideation is the process of shaping these flurries of thoughts into something we can use. Journaling is planting the seeds of ideas that later blossom into actions.

R — Reading

What do you want to learn? What do you want to explore? By investing in reading five pages a day, you could expand your knowledge with roughly a book every month. Not only will this help you learn about specific subjects or gain life perspectives, but research shows reading can positively change your brain structure. Reading is one of the best antidotes to the mindless phone scrolling that consumes so much of our time.

A — Analyzation

A vital step in the idea and execution process is analyzing the results, not through breaking down a complex database of information, but through introspection. How do we feel about what happened? What would we do again, and what would we avoid in the future? Nelson Mandela once said, "I never lose—I either win or learn." Analyzation is taking the time to learn from what we've done. With that approach, we can take comfort because we never really make mistakes.

C — Calmness

I believe we can all agree that panic rarely improves a situation. Although, at times, the feeling can feel unavoidable. One way to counter panic during challenging circumstances is to remind ourselves of when we faced similar situations in the past and persevered. It's another form of mind talk—when we take a moment to tell ourselves, "You got this, [insert your name]." You got this.

L — Listening

Usually, when we think of the importance of listening, it's about listening to others, which is vital in communication and conflict resolution with the people in our lives. But I want to highlight another critical aspect—listening to ourselves. That gut feeling we all have is compelling. It's easy to forget we are our own best advisors. So, I encourage you to take a moment and listen to your own mind when tasked with making a decision. Then take the appropriate action. After all, there's no other human on the planet we'll spend more time with than ourselves. So, let's invest time in listening to ourselves, which will lead to designing our lives.

E — Exercise

I want to emphasize the importance of thinking small again. This is not about changing our entire schedules, signing up for a marathon, or cranking out bench presses in the gym. Dedicating five minutes—stretching, doing jump jacks, a brisk walk, anything—is a relatively easy way to begin our days with positivity. You'll never regret the time, no matter how short, you give to exercise. My son Yuvaan keeps me on my toes and makes me play with him for at least 15-20 minutes daily.

S — Silence

We are surrounded by noise: the physical kind, such as traffic, the constant dinging of phones, and the noise in our minds. The human brain processes about 60,000 to 80,000 thoughts daily—that's an awful lot of noise. Allowing five minutes a day (you may notice a pattern emerging) of uninterrupted silence can profoundly affect our mental and physical health. It will enable us to reflect, helping us fight against our body's response to stress. Through connecting with ourselves in this quiet way, we can better connect with the world around us.

I believe in the power of HABITS4MIRACLES to transform ourselves and, in the process, transform our society. The National Alliance on Mental Illness says that 20% of Americans are dealing with the problem of mental illness. And 12 million have had serious thoughts of committing suicide.

Here is my request: if in the last 10 minutes you had positive thoughts flowing in your mind, thinking these habits could benefit your family, friends, and coworkers, please enlighten them by sharing this book.

Here are some ideas for you to practice and habits to incorporate into your daily routine:

- Start writing down your thoughts, feelings, and opinions, as it helps you to better listen to yourself. Keep a journal or use an app like Reflectly, Happyfeed or a five-minute journal.

- Have you ever been stuck and unable to get ideas for moving forward? I have found that putting your brain in "active mode" by going for a walk, taking a shower, or swimming brings many new ideas. (I generate a lot of ideas while swimming!)

- "Vigorous reading," especially personal development books, makes a difference. Please ensure you do the exercises the author suggests, pause every so often, and ask yourself, "How might that apply in my life?"

- Review the names of people in your Inner Circle; are they the people who are encouraging, motivating, and bring positive energy to you? If that is not the case, it is time for you to change or add new people to your circle.

- Self-Care—Most often, we support the needs of others: spouses, significant others, children, coworkers, and our manager. When was the last time you did something for yourself? We neglect self-care, and for me, that is our biggest challenge. Start spending time with yourself, do things you love, and which will make you happy, PERIOD.

Incorporating these kinds of practices into what we do every day may save lives and help us manage our mental health. Our actions can influence our loved ones to do the same. I can't think of a better way to serve our community than this.

Let me take you back to my college days, around the time when I started smoking. My roommate had landed a job where he was responsible for collaborating with and promoting a newly launched cigarette brand. He had many stocks available, and one of those two voices in my head made me cave in. I felt it had impacted my health to a great extent, and I had to stop. For almost a year, I tried to trick myself into quitting through many techniques, such as not keeping cigarettes around or not buying them anymore. I also tried other ways to stop, but could only resist for so long. I finally engaged in some inner dialogue and went to a temple to ask God to grant me the strength to break the habit. I think it was the 27th of March 2011 when I smoked last, and that made me believe in mind talk. It made me think that if I could do it once, I could do it again, no matter what situation I was stuck in. Smoking is an issue with which many people struggle, and trust me when I tell you, with mind talk, you can quit it.

As we move along this journey, you can take a proactive step towards self-growth by engaging in these activities:

1. Each morning, as soon as you get out of bed, think of one thing you would like to achieve that day.
2. Think about how accomplishing that one thing would move you towards your life goals.

Once you are comfortable doing that one thing daily, move it to two and three. And along the journey, you will fail—not to fall, but to rise again.

If you like what I'm sharing here, please visit www.Habits4Miracles.com/jumpstart and download your free eBook, "5 Steps on How to Take Consistent Action to Get What You Want." On that page, I also share additional resources just for those of you reading this book. Here's to changing your habits for good!

About the Author

Rahul Sharma

Rahul Sharma is an accomplished Learning and Development Professional from Northern Virginia. He holds an MBA in Human Resources and a master's degree in Organization Development. His background includes transforming business operations and people by clearly identifying the root cause, championing a client-focused mindset, and fostering a firm commitment to resolving issues. In his leisure time, Rahul spends time with his kids, plays Sudoku, enjoys swimming, and takes every opportunity to learn new things.

Jumpstart Your Healing Choices

Demystifying Eastern/Western Medicine

By Carol Rudd

We make thousands of choices every day: what time to wake up, which clothes to wear, what foods to eat, what schools to attend, whom to marry, and even the route to take to work. Which is the best option, the cheapest, the most environmentally friendly? Even when you hit a roadblock or a detour in your journey, I'm here to tell you that you always have a choice!

I want to talk to you about healing choices, and why awareness of our choices is so important.

I grew up in a small Midwestern town and came from German heritage. The messages I inherited were, "Life is hard," "You have to pull yourself up by your own bootstraps," and "There's no such thing as a free lunch." And I believed those axioms. I struggled to breathe with asthma as a child, and I truly felt the evidence that life was hard.

Then, on my first job out of high school as a telephone operator, my supervisor changed my life path. I was a hormonal, frustrated young adult and my supervisor was a high-energy, bubbly woman who smiled all the time. One day outside of work, in my frustration, I blurted out, "How can you be so happy all the time!?" She laughed and said, "I choose to be happy." And that was a mind-blowing, life-altering statement that has reverberated throughout my life!

We get to choose every moment of every day, how we want to be in the world! So many people don't realize that they are "in charge" of their lives! They drift along, letting circumstances direct their paths. They "go with the flow, let nature take its course," and worst of all, they let others choose for them.

Who am I? I'm Carol Rudd, a retired respiratory therapist, and an asthmatic since age three. I have worked and lived with people who struggle to breathe. I truly know the panic and fear of breathlessness. I also know the embarrassment and feelings of hopelessness that come when you can't do the things you love. So, I'm writing to talk about choices—Healing Choices—and why it's my mission to provide healing choices to those with breathing problems.

Many people, my mom included, get stuck when it comes to the idea of quitting smoking. They may have tried once or twice and failed, so they give up—they say they can't quit—when in reality they have chosen not to try any more. Choice means continuing to take the steps to get the results you want. It's not a one-and-done kind of thing. In every moment of the day, you need to choose that cigarettes are not good for you; you must choose to repeatedly say no to those urges. Healing choices around addictions are hard because the urges are subconscious, and we have to make them conscious. Keeping your reason/motivation at the top of your mind and gaining clarity around what and why you are choosing is essential. Often, the motivation needs to be life-threatening before a person is clearly able to see the choice. Consistently choosing those things that support life are healing choices, and is the Ultimate Gift we give ourselves.

What makes a choice a "healing" choice? Think about the cancer patient, choosing chemotherapy or radiation. Or what about the person on the other end of the same procedure who refuses to do anything more to save their life? Either can be (and usually is) the healing choice, even though it may not feel like it to the rest of the family. Healing choices are about the whole person, being grounded in who they are and listening to that tiny voice always.

I learned about the power of words and chose positive energy words like love, joy, hope, and action words like “get to,” or “choose to,” rather than “have to,” or “need to.”

When I worked full time, I noticed how negative my coworkers were about anything and everything. I would join in on the “pity party,” and I felt drained by all the complaining and hate-filled words. I started avoiding those people who were most noticeably pulling me into their misery. Shortly thereafter, I read a book on the power of our words, and I worked to eliminate those disempowering words from my vocabulary. I used to say this or that was “killing me,” or “I hate” something, and I realized I did not want to choose those outcomes. Now, I strongly dislike something or some behavior, but I don’t hate anything or anybody!

I recall one time when my mom was hospitalized. I had driven four hours to be with her, and I was going to meet up with my dad first for a bite to eat. But he left the house without me, and I didn’t know where he was, or where my mom was. I was furious at my dad, as there was a lot more to the story, but that was the night I made one of my first healing choices. I chose to forgive my dad for his impatience and insensitivity. My reasoning was that my anger wasn’t hurting him; it was only hurting me to hold on to my anger.

I learned three valuable lessons that day:

1. My dad was not the perfect person who I thought he was.
2. Anger eats you up and is very toxic, with little impact on the person you're angry at.
3. Letting go of anger doesn't mean you condone another's behavior; rather, you love them enough to forgive them.

Here's another example of a healing choice. I used to be an impatient driver, irritated by others' lack of respect for fellow drivers. I'd even experienced road rage when a guy in a truck who was in the right lane next to me made a left turn in front of me and almost cut me off completely. I was so angry; I chased him down the hill and back up the next hill, cussing and honking my horn. I was blind with rage. We reached the top of the hill and neared an upcoming red light. Suddenly I thought, what if he gets out of his truck? Or worse, what if he has a club or a gun? Luckily, the light changed to green, and I vowed I would never again allow myself to lose emotional control while driving.

Demystifying Eastern/Western Medicine

Doctors and patients both rely heavily on quick fixes or "Band-Aids" for symptom relief rather than seeking real cures for any ailment. The pharmaceutical companies see to it that we have prescriptions and over-the-counter medicines for every ache and pain! Don't misunderstand me, Western medicine has its place and is especially good in emergency situations and life-or-death circumstances like car accidents, heart attacks, or strokes. However, in most cases, it seems we have lost our desire to do what it takes to be healthy.

As an adult, I have searched out many alternative wellness solutions. My primary focus has been traditional Chinese medicine (TCM), or Eastern medicine, which takes a whole different approach to healthcare. The key word is "whole." TCM looks at the whole person, not just the symptom (such as a sore shoulder or knee). And yes, today there are some functional medicine doctors who take a holistic approach as well, but they are not the majority.

Much of a medical doctor's training involves learning about the medicines that are available to treat a disease. What they need to understand is that there is no benefit to the drug companies to create medicines that actually "cure" people. They are "in it" for long-term customers who need their pills. What's even worse is that, by law, pharmaceutical companies cannot use anything "natural" in their products. So, they take natural ingredients and alter them so they are no longer natural. That is why so many pharmaceutical drugs have unpleasant or even harmful side effects.

Eastern medicine, on the other hand, uses natural herbal products and substances that are gentler and in alignment with the flow of your body systems—and they don't cause negative side effects. There is no quick fix with Eastern medicine supplements; you just have to be patient and listen to your body.

The complexity and simplicity of traditional Chinese medicine fascinated me. For starters, TCM practitioners look at the whole person, including pulse, tongue and face color, nutrition, sleep, sound of voice, and even smell. They also look at the seasons and have beautiful descriptors and analogies for each. For example, fall is a season of dryness (think brittle leaves), the essential organ is the lung, the nonessential organ is the skin, the color is white or pale, and the emotion is grief or sorrow. Interestingly, people with breathing problems often have skin problems, too. There are many other correlations, but the point is, there is a depth and understanding that TCM brings to healing choices.

I was initially drawn to Eastern medicine through Tai Chi. Then, I began exploring AMMA Therapy (a form of Asian bodywork that follows the energy pathways). I had experienced nothing like it before. I'd had massages, deep tissue and Swedish, but AMMA Therapy has an energy focus rather than a "meat tenderizer" or muscular focus. By getting energy moving through the body, people can learn what it's like to be grounded. To get out of those ever-swirling thoughts and emotions and just be present in my physical body—it was life-changing for me! I experienced an inner calm for the first time, and I knew I wanted to learn AMMA after my first session.

In my study of Chinese medicine, I learned how our emotions are linked to organ systems and how traumas of any kind can lock emotions into our bodies. These locked-in emotions can create energy blockages and ultimately lead to dis-ease. The form of massage I offer works energetically to release blockages and get your energy moving, thereby promoting healing. I used to be a "stuffer" of emotions, holding everything inside. I was teased for being a "crybaby" and experienced lots of traumas in childhood.

Qigong is all about grounding yourself and being in your physical body. Your heart is your emotional center, your head is your mental center, and below your belly button is your physical center. When the nebulousness of your thoughts and emotions gets too large, you become less grounded and can lose yourself. The goal is to become more grounded in your physical being, to balance out and become the best person you can be.

By Carol Rudd

Here is one last story about healing choice. When I was in my early 20's, I had a boyfriend for about one year. We would go out to the bars and travel together, mostly doing activities he wanted to do, but rarely doing what I enjoyed. I was young, on my own, and not really sure what love was all about. Christmas came and went, and my birthday came and went. There was no present, no acknowledgement of his affection, even when he'd gotten a gift from me. So, one day shortly after my birthday, I asked him why he'd never gotten me a gift. His response was, "At least I don't beat you." I was shocked! And I dumped him on the spot. Healing choice: I deserved love and respect! This was another pivotal point in my life. I realized the threat, and I chose myself! I now have deep wisdom and a strong sense of self. I know what I want, and I am now married to a wonderful man who loves and cares for me every day!

Taking steps or making choices that are positive and life-affirming are healing choices!

I'm a huge fan of Mike Dooley and his "Notes from the Universe" (Google him). He basically says what you think about, you create. We spend a lot of time mentally and emotionally thinking about bills, health concerns, or negative possibilities. The more we think, worry, or work ourselves into anxiety, it's likely we'll get more of the same.

Making positive healing choices requires:

1. Listening to your soul: that quiet, small voice
2. Being conscious of your words and thoughts
3. Stopping or minimizing the negative self-talk
4. Re-evaluating beliefs or subconscious behaviors
5. Learning or relearning what brings you joy
6. Thinking and speaking about what you want rather than what you don't want

So, choice starts with a belief in yourself, that sense of worthiness and deservedness that we sometimes take a long time to learn. Knowing that you are always in *choice* gives you room to pivot your mind and allows grace for any wrong turns or roadblocks along the way. No matter how many wrong choices we've made in our lives, there is always that next choice that can turn things around. Be your healing choice!

To learn more about me, my Qigong practice, lung support services, and/or just to connect, please go to www.HealingChoicesOasis.com/jumpstart.

About the Author

Carol Rudd

Carol is a licensed massage therapist and respiratory therapist with 41 years in healthcare. She combines the best of Eastern and Western medicine through AMMA Therapy, Qigong, and Western-based education and exercise for those with lung diseases (COPD). She brings a wealth of knowledge and insights to her practice, with programs for adults and kids alike. Carol's mission is to offer hope, joy, and healing to those seeking wellness.

Jumpstart Your Ideal Lifestyle

Getting More Love in Your Life & Money in Your Business

By Katrina Sawa

So, let's talk about first things first. What does your current life look like and feel like?

Are you totally and completely happy with every aspect of your life?

If not, what's missing? What doesn't feel right? In which areas do you wish things were different?

I'm not trying to depress you here. Hopefully, your life is going pretty well at this point. However, in my experience working with thousands of entrepreneurs over the years, especially women, I've found that most are NOT completely happy.

Are you completely happy and in love with your significant other, or are you settling in your relationship? Are you hoping it will get better, waiting for them to change, or thinking it will work itself out?

If you currently do not have a significant other, do you either wish you did or are you still hurting from a previous relationship?

I believe that having this kind of love in your life is essential to anyone who desires success or happiness in life or business. This isn't to say that you can never be happy without a significant other. Your love life is definitely somewhere we want to focus. In fact, it could be the crucial element for you, like it was for me.

On top of what's happening in your love life, we also want to examine your career or business life; this is the other part of your life in which you spend the most time. Are you settling in a job you hate, or working hard for bosses who under-value you? Do you have your own business, but you're barely surviving financially?

I believe that to have your most ideal lifestyle, you want to have a very happy love side of your life and an extremely profitable and satisfying career or business side of your life. (I like to call it the "money side," so you want to focus on love and money.) And of course, you might be thinking, "What about my family and friends?" Those fall into the "love side" too. Hear me out...

When I first left the corporate world and entered entrepreneurship, I was married to my "starter husband." I thought my husband at the time had an entrepreneurial spirit, since we had met doing door-to-door sales. I figured that, because he was willing to do that kind of outgoing, self-motivated type of sales, he would understand me wanting to run my business and have more flexibility in life.

I found out quickly, though, that he had many more concerns for our financial security than I had expected. You see, I always knew I would become an entrepreneur at some point in my life. I had that feeling from an early age. I just didn't know what I would be doing until the point when I actually quit my final job.

I had been seeing a business coach for a few months prior to leaving my job, because I still felt a bit confused as to what kind of business I would start. I had a few different ideas, but I wasn't totally sure about any of them. Looking back on it, some fears had crept in, too. I was scared to choose the wrong type of business and fail at it, or not make any money. I was unsure of my own abilities, or how to position myself to potential prospects.

So, where are you in the process of becoming an entrepreneur? Are you already one, and loving life? If so, great! But what's still missing? Is it the money, the six-, seven-, or eight-figure income that you're still waiting to achieve?

Or are you just starting out and determined to make it work, but you aren't sure exactly HOW to do it the right way? In my other chapter in this book, Jumpstart Your New Business, I show you how to make fewer mistakes, spend less money up front, and clarify what you are meant to do on this planet.

There is a definite way to structure your business and your life to create your ideal lifestyle. In my mind, having both love and money is the key to extreme happiness and success. Not only can you and your family then have whatever you desire, but you can also serve or contribute to countless more people.

It's time for YOU.

Take a moment now to outline what you want your ultimate lifestyle to look like. I hope you design it around what you truly want, not just about what others around you want or think you should have.

You need to take care of YOU first. Put YOU first, then your family, then your clients, and then everyone else. You won't be any good to anyone around you—kids, significant other, clients, family—unless you take care of YOUR needs first.

I'm not just talking about a massage and facial once a month, either. I'm talking about taking care of the inner you.

This means:

- Nurturing your thoughts and feelings.
- Expressing your passions and desires.
- Discovering your true, authentic self.
- Developing your inner wisdom, peace, and purpose.
- Allowing yourself to grow, feel, and be one with God in order to be of service to those you are meant to serve and inspire.

Now, don't get freaked out by that last statement about God. I'm not trying to get religious on you here, but finding a connection to a higher source will help you on your journey to becoming who you need to be.

This is what happened for me.

About a year and a half into my business transformation from the old model to the new one, I'd done all I could do to move the business forward. I'd implemented all the ideas and strategies that my mentors had suggested. I'd marketed the way I knew how to market, but the big money still wasn't coming to me.

I couldn't figure out why. I was very frustrated, as you can imagine. I'd put in all the hard work, long hours, and money, but it was taking forever to get the income level where I wanted it to be. Maybe you can relate?

I was in a business mastermind group at the time, which was basically a group of my friends and peers. They kept telling me to "Stop doing more," and to "Just be yourself." I didn't get it at first, and I began getting frustrated. "What the heck do they mean?" I thought.

For months, I struggled with these thoughts of "just being" or "being LOVE" they used to say to me repeatedly. I didn't know what that meant. I was the "just do it" girl; my claim to fame was that I got things done. I was an implementer.

What I found out after some soul-searching and many months of one-on-one coaching with my mentor was that I wasn't being my true, authentic self.

Instead, I was trying to be this person with this great business and talent. The only way I can describe it is that it was "all on the outside." I was wearing a mask, it seemed. There was something about myself I didn't want to let out.

YOU are the key to happiness.

Through many months of coaching, self-development, and business conferences, I met more and more people who seemed to have this "inner work stuff" all figured out. They were inspirational to me. I believe I manifested them into my life to help me learn how to bring out the real me.

During this time, my husband and I decided to call it quits. It was a pretty amicable split and mutual decision, luckily for me. I didn't have to go through a big, ugly divorce, like many of my friends had. My ex and I basically realized that we had gone down different paths in life and grown apart. He was more into a corporate position where he enjoyed the security of a monthly paycheck, and I was definitely into the less stable, yet more fascinating world of entrepreneurship.

What we learned from the experience is that neither of us was happy anymore. We had lost the passion for each other as well, and were basically just roommates toward the end. We decided that we both wanted to be happy and we deserved to be happy and in love again, but to do that, we'd be better off apart.

Many of my clients and friends and their significant others don't see eye to eye. Some think about divorcing, while others try to stay and hope things get better. Either way, divorce is not a fun thing, but if you're truly not happy and you and your significant other are truly on different life paths, then why suffer?

Besides, I'm a product of a divorce and I turned out just fine. I'm very well-balanced and open to self-development–LOOK! And now I'm married to an amazing man, and he came with a very special three-and-a-half-year-old, Riley, who is now 13. And while it was hard for her from about age 5 to age 10, she now realizes how good she has it with two families that are happy instead of one that is not. Having kids is not a reason to stay if you're being abused or unloved; they see what's happening.

Getting divorced is one of the best things I did for myself. I became totally free the day I decided to leave—free from the negative pull that he had on my energy, and more. Your environment and the people you hang around with every day or every week affect who you are, what you think, and how you interact with everyone, including your clients.

Who is someone you see often, for example, who always drains your energy? They need you to listen to them, their problems, their drama, or the negative stories that come out of their mouths.

Who is someone who criticizes what you do? Who questions your business savvy? Who makes you feel uncomfortable when discussing your business goals or achievements?

If you have people in your life who do these things, talk down to you, or even worse, tell you flat-out, “You can’t do it,” or, “You will only fail,” how do you think they are affecting your business or your job, and especially your self-confidence? You must protect your environment, your positive energy, your self-esteem, and your self-confidence. Without a hundred percent self-confidence, do you really believe you’ll ever achieve your highest goals?

Probably not.

Lack of confidence in even the smallest or most insignificant way, a way in which you may not even notice, is one of the major reasons I see small businesses fail—or fail to launch.

Make the commitment.

Now that you’ve discovered some things about yourself that you may not have been aware of before, it’s time to commit to changing them. You should make at least a small commitment to yourself now that you will be open to change. Define what’s most important to you and what your ultimate lifestyle looks like.

Then, identify what your true, authentic self looks like, what you care about, what matters to you, and how you want to continue living your life each day. If this doesn’t look like the way you are currently living your life now, then make the decision to do some work to change it.

It is all right for you to put yourself first. It is okay for you to make changes towards making yourself a better person. This is not selfish. This is selfless, because when you are happier, you will be a much better person, which means you will be a better wife, mother, and businessperson.

But first you must DECIDE to make a commitment to yourself to do whatever it takes. My other book, *Love Yourself Successful*, covers this idea in depth.

But regardless of what I say here and what small steps or actions you may take, without complete commitment, you may not succeed.

Take action now.

The only action I want you to take at this point is to make the decision to put yourself first from here forward. This is the first step.

Choose not to surround yourself with any negative forces, people, or events. (Stop listening to negative news and media stories too, if it helps!)

Listen to the inner voice inside you when it tells you to take time out or to treat yourself.

Allow yourself to satisfy your needs before the needs of others (obviously, except for emergencies or for your children, to some extent).

Set uncomfortably big goals.

Money goals, love goals, and life goals: these are what you want to set up every year, or every month, if you prefer. I challenge you to think bigger. Think of other things I haven't mentioned too—what matters to you?

Raise those money goals; triple them if you have to. You don't have to know HOW it will happen, but if you can think of a higher number, write that down instead. Shoot, if you're an entrepreneur like I am, you can make as much money as you want—it's limitless!

Are you committed to being a little uncomfortable for a while to achieve this fantastic new lifestyle and business that makes you so happy you could scream?

Design your ultimate lifestyle.

I previously asked you to describe what you wanted your ultimate lifestyle to look like. But do you now have a slightly different picture?

It's okay to have it all: the money, the love, and the complete happiness. If those around you don't believe it's possible or acknowledge that you deserve it, then surround yourself with different people!

Realize and know deep down inside that it is okay for you to be happy, have all the money you want, and be more successful than anyone you know. There is more out there for you if you decide you want it.

I found a way to be totally and completely happy in my life and my career, to have love within myself and in my relationships, and to experience the money rolling in like never before. I know hundreds of friends, clients, and peers who have also done this. But it takes work.

Mostly, it takes work on the inside to adjust your beliefs, your thoughts, and your decision to want more. The “doing” part is the easy part; I can show you that later. Seriously though, if you’re trying to boost your business and make more money, all the marketing in the world doesn’t matter without the right mindset about love and money.

I encourage you to dig deep into your heart and soul to discover what you truly want in life and figure out who you want to be.

If you want to learn how to grow and scale a more profitable business, I invite you to take my Jumpstart Your Biz Quiz online at www.JumpstartYourBizQuiz.com**. And if you want to jumpstart the love side of your life**, go check out some resources I have from a different book I wrote that can help you put yourself first, go to www.JumpstartYourLoveLife.net.

About the Author

Katrina Sawa

Katrina is the creator of The Jumpstart Your Business in 90 Days System, the International Speaker Network, and she's an International Best-Selling author of *Jumpstart Your New Business Now, Love Yourself Successful, and 18 other books.* She's been featured on the Oprah and Friends XMRadio Network, ABC, and TheCW. Katrina loves to inspire and educate entrepreneurs on how to create a consistent money-making business doing what they love.

Jumpstart Your Money Mindset

3 Keys to Rewriting Your Limiting Beliefs Around Money

By Nicole J. Aspenson

If you are not where you would like to be regarding your finances, I understand. I have been there! At age 40, I was broke and always stressed about paying bills. I would roll change to go grocery shopping. I took a list and a calculator to the store with me, and I often cried all the way home from the stress.

In addition, I watched my mom lose half of her 401k two years before she intended to retire. What do you think my vision of 'retirement' was at that time? "I'll NEVER be able to retire. I'll work every day the rest of my life until I die."

As many women do, I became lost; we are busy juggling work, family, and school. In my case, I was also raising a special needs child. I had low self-esteem. I felt helpless because of limiting beliefs that held me back. I was in a toxic marriage, and I didn't feel confident that I could support my son and myself. So, I remained "stuck."

In 2011, I was invited to Wine, Women & Wealth. I had no idea how much this community would change my life.

I discovered remarkable leaders and mentors who empowered me to find myself again and step into my power and my passion. Eventually, I became strong enough to hold space for others to do the same.

I saw the crusade to empower and educate everyday Americans, especially women, about how money works, and I knew I wanted to be part of this life-changing organization. I realized I could support myself and my son both emotionally and financially. After gaining the courage to get divorced, I spent the next year working hard on myself and building my business.

Only three years after the divorce, I was making a six-figure income. I experienced all-expenses-paid, five-star reward trips and leadership retreats. And I found a kind, supportive gentleman who is now my husband.

I love teaching money principles to families, small business owners, successful singles, and corporate executives who desire to take charge of their financial futures so they can have financial freedom.

I am excited that I have an opportunity to help women take control of their finances so that they will not feel stuck in any situation. At Wine, Women and Wealth, I get to encourage women to rewrite their money mindsets and rewrite old stories that are not serving them. We get to have vulnerable, heartfelt conversations about money and Money Mindset with zero judgement. Women can find community, learn about money, seek encouragement, and be uplifted together.

Whether it's at one of our classes or in a one-on-one conversation, I get to share about Money Mindset. You are likely to discover some old "stuff!" When you were born, you were a blank slate. You learned from the people around you and the experiences you had. Some beliefs were gifted to you and set in your unconscious mind before you matured and before you could filter them.

Did you know that by age seven, children have already set the habits that will help them manage their money?

Between the ages of two and seven years old, you soaked up everything the surrounding adults were saying and doing. The adults were writing your story. You may have heard things like, "Don't touch the stove or you will get burned," "The rich get richer while the poor get poorer," or "Money doesn't grow on trees." Those who saw their parents fighting over money learned, "If I make money or talk about money, I'll get yelled at." Your mind did not know whether to trust what the adults told you or to follow your own perceptions about what was true.

All the pre-programming before age seven affects the way you think about and view the world. Your thoughts drive your habits, which determine results. It is an ongoing cycle. Positive thoughts lead to good habits, creating good results. And it works the same way in the negative.

The good news is that you can be aware of those thoughts. You can work on paying attention to the old messages that pop up and rewrite them. Now that you are an adult, you get to write your story. And now you can reason, question, and reevaluate which beliefs are not serving you. You can choose to master your Money Mindset.

First, notice any limiting thoughts and beliefs.

Second, investigate and be curious about where a limiting belief came from. Journal about it. Recall what your parents told you about rich people or wealth. What did neighbors say? What did the media show?

Once you investigate, you can question the thoughts. Ask, "Is that absolutely true?" Let's say you heard that all rich people are corrupt and greedy. Well, do you know at least one wealthy person who is generous and kind? Could you think of another? Now you can rewrite that limiting belief. This is an ongoing process; you'll knock down a belief and it will come back and test you again, allowing you to anchor in the new belief.

Here is an example of what a client might say: "I want to save $500 a month for 30 years for retirement." When I do my homework to find a strategy that will allow them to achieve that goal, I can give that $500 a path to become wealth, rather than have it go down the drain on frivolous spending.

Another Money Mindset conversation involves having a budget. How did that word make you feel? Did you cringe? Did old beliefs pop up?

The question is, what is the actual purpose of having a budget?

A budget is simply a tool, even though 'budget' has sometimes been misconstrued as a punishment. If the word 'budget' makes you cringe, then rename it! Would you like a spending plan, or a saving guide? If you think of a budget as something to look back on and punish yourself over, you might as well not even have one. However, if a budget becomes a tool, and you know that once a month you need a lunch with friends or a massage, you build that into the budget. You plan for it!

Are you balancing spending with saving? Having a goal makes your daily spending choices easier. Add a vacation fund to your budget. If you're saving for a Mediterranean cruise, it's easier not to spend on things you don't need today.

Does your money run out before the month's end? You can navigate by refinancing your finances. Evaluate where your money is going. Assess items like home and auto insurance, taxes, your 401k. When you recognize how money is being misappropriated in your budget, you can adjust the budget to start your savings plan or future spending plan. Know where your money is going and where you might adjust. And you may "find" money to create the financial future of your dreams.

In our Money 101 class, we teach the concept of saving $5 a day. Do you think you could save $5 a day? Most say yes, as a knee-jerk reaction. And then they do the math. They figure out that $5 a day comes out to about $150 a month. Often, they claim there's no way they could save $150 a month. It is simply a matter of mindset, emotion vs. logic. One key step to Money Mindset is to understand your emotions about money. Then, follow logic and mathematics. Did you know that $150 a month for 40 years earning 8% would turn into over $500,000? Yes, that one is for the twenty-somethings. If you do not have 40 years before retirement, it may take a little more than $5 a day. A simple compound interest calculator can help you do the math.

What lifestyle would you like to create? Get really clear on your dreams and have specific objectives. Next, ask a financial professional to help you determine a path to get from here to there. If you have clear objectives, it will help to have a productive conversation with your financial professional.

Another mistake people make is not setting up a foundation for their financial household. Unfortunately, most people often start in risk and never set up a foundation. Without a foundation, your financial household could collapse, like it did for 71% of Americans in 2008. It is your safety net. It comprises your insurance policies, your safe money strategies, Living Benefits, and guaranteed lifetime income. This is money that you know will be there to support financial freedom in your future.

Warren Buffett has two rules:

> "Rule No. 1 is never lose money.
> Rule No. 2 is never forget Rule No. 1."

You may wonder, "How do I never lose money?"

Did you know you do not have to lose money in your retirement accounts? I enjoy teaching my clients how they can gain the upside potential in the market while protecting from the downside. Yes, that means when the market is up, their account goes up and, most importantly, when the market is down, they never lose a dime because of the market. It's not just about what you make, it's about what you keep!

Speaking of what you keep, did you know you can create a retirement plan where you do not have to share your money with Uncle Sam? There are vehicles that allow you to contribute after taxes, grow your money non-taxed, and access your money tax-free! Most people are aware of a Roth IRA; however, many do not fully understand the limitations. You can only contribute up to a limit. The IRS will penalize you if you withdraw any money prior to age 59 ½, and if you make too much money, you are not allowed to contribute to a Roth IRA at all. One of my favourite vehicles is a Tax-Free Indexed Account. It works like a Roth IRA on steroids. You have all the tax-free benefits with none of the limitations.

Another barrier people put in their own way is avoiding the habit of saving. Starting small now—and we are talking really small—is going to help "future you" be in a much better place down the line. Just one or two years of missed savings can hurt more than you may think. If you start saving when you're 29 instead of 27, your retirement nest egg could literally be tens of thousands of dollars smaller once you reach age 65. That's because of the power of compound interest; your money multiplies faster the longer you've had it in an interest-accruing account, because you're getting paid interest on your interest.

Let me ask you to think about your most important asset. What came to mind? Your home? Your health is your most important asset. If you are not covered for the "just in case" things that could happen to you, it could be devastating financially. Yes, I am talking about life insurance. Hang on... I'm talking about the new kind of life insurance, the kind that you do not have to die to use.

Did you know:

- According to a 2019 study by the American Heart Association, a stroke occurs every 40 seconds in the U.S.
- Also in 2019, the Centers for Disease Control and Prevention reports that 6 in 10 Americans live with at least one chronic disease.
- Approximately 530,000 bankruptcies are filed annually because of medical debt, according to the American Public Health Association in 2019.

Life insurance with living benefits is a valuable financial planning tool. Living Benefits life insurance gives you the power to accelerate your death benefit while you're still living if you suffer from stroke, heart attack, cancer diagnosis, or critical, chronic, or terminal illness.

Finally, let me ask you to imagine what retirement looks like for you. Our grandparents had seven to ten years left after retirement. You may need to plan for 25 to 30 years of pay checks when you retire. It might be time to redefine "retirement." Perhaps it looks like working two or three days per week instead of five or six. Maybe you'll take off every Friday to be with grandchildren. Or you might take three months off a year to travel.

I invite you to spend time thinking about your Golden Years and give yourself permission to dream about what you want those years to look like! Having this vision makes it much easier to create a financial plan that will support your lifestyle. It certainly makes your day-to-day choices of spending and saving easier if you have a vision to look forward to. And most importantly, when you are clear about your budget, your dreams and goals, and your risk tolerance, you and your financial professional can cultivate a collaborative relationship rather than a parent/child-type relationship.

I realize this is a lot of information, so I have put together a page on my website for you to see how you can learn more, see Living Benefit testimonials, view invitations to our events, and find out how to receive **a free eBook of Wine, Women & Wealth.** Reach out and let's have a conversation! Go to www.NicoleAspenson.com/jumpstart.

About the Author

Nicole J. Aspenson

Nicole is passionate about financial education. From business owners to business executives, from families to successful singles, she enjoys helping clients reach their financial goals. Nicole is a Financial Strategist, speaker, author, and an expert at gathering resources for her clients. Whether you want to take control of your finances or are interested in a career helping others achieve their financial dreams, contact Nicole to Anchor Your Financial Freedom!

Jumpstart Your Wealth

3 Places to Get Started Today

By Anna Felix

It was the one-year anniversary of the passing of my father, and my daughter and I were reminiscing. I had piled the photo albums high around us. Some were lying open to specific pages, and others were waiting to be opened. Images of my family, my childhood, and our friends had evoked so many emotions: gratitude, longing, serenity, and so much love.

During the past decade, we had lost my husband (her father), and both of my parents (her grandparents). It was beautiful to realize that, even though we deeply missed our loved ones, we were blessed with the kind of riches that money can't buy: unconditional love, respect, and care. Our hearts were full, and I felt so grateful to have experienced the things portrayed in all those pictures.

I consider myself wealthy and rich in so many areas of my life today, but it wasn't that long ago that I realized I needed to change my mindset around money and all things financial. I needed to jumpstart my wealth, do a "reboot," initiate a "do-over," or whatever phraseology denotes getting the train going down the "right" track.

If you've had a similar feeling in the past, or are experiencing it right now, I invite you to take a little stroll with me down Money Lane. I'm going to share with you a few pivotal things I've learned that I know will change the financial trajectory of your life.

Key Smart Money Lessons of the Wealthy

Let's start with lessons that we can learn from those who have been savvy and smart with their money. There are philosophies, ways of doing things, and strategies that the wealthy have embraced, and anyone desirous of more can do the same.

- Start saving and investing early
- Accumulate a lot of money, but don't always earn a lot
- Live modestly—below their earnings
- Spend frugally on items they need

- Invest first and spend what's left
- Invest in income-producing assets (i.e., businesses, real estate, the stock market, etc.)
- Show worth through relationships and meaningful possessions
- Earn income by working for themselves
- Invest to create income streams and passive income
- Borrow only for capital investments or property, i.e., home, business, etc.

It may not be possible to implement all these steps immediately, but being aware of what works provides a starting place, and over time, we can add these strategies to our journey down Money Lane. Did you notice a common theme? Being aware of where money is being spent and making wise investments are priorities. Financial success is not a hard science. It's a soft skill, where behavior is more important than knowledge. It might be surprising to you, but an awareness of your thoughts about money is the best place to start.

Create a Money Mindset

To achieve the wealth you desire, you must create a winning Money Mindset. What is a Money Mindset? Your Money Mindset is unique to you. It includes your beliefs, attitudes, and feelings about money. It drives every decision you make about your finances, including spending, saving, and investing. It can also affect your inner peace, your ability to sleep, and even the joy you experience in your life.

People with a healthy Money Mindset believe things like:

- I deserve to be wealthy.
- I attract my desired goal.
- I am enough.

In this book, there is a chapter that does a deeper dive into your mindset. I encourage you to use the information that Nicole Aspenson shares about removing blocks and creating the future you desire by managing your mindset.

While mindset is a critical first step to success, the winning formula combines two other elements. Your results are magical when you add strategy and execution. Create affirmations that focus on what you want versus what you don't want. If you have a partner, substitute, "My partner and I..." when you're repeating your affirmations:

- I am enough.
- I am financially free.
- I deserve wealth.
- I invest with ease.

Set Clear Long-Term Financial Goals

Wealthy individuals know where they are going because they have clearly defined goals. When you have goals, boulders won't deter you. When you don't, pebbles will wreak havoc on your journey.

As you set your goals, it's important to visualize your dream life. The power of visualizing your future and what you want is one of the most powerful skills you can develop to remove blocks and attract what you desire.

Develop habits that support your dream. The secret is to clarify what you want and then consistently execute. Don't beat yourself up when you get off course; just get back on course. Over time, you will develop new beliefs that will affect your behaviors and actions and ultimately improve your results.

Reduce Debts and Expenses

Obviously, it is ideal for you to be as close to debt-free as possible, but the savvy money hack involves using debt when it makes sense. Use other people's money to fund something that will initiate your own wealth accumulation, such as a mortgage, a business loan, or a real estate opportunity.

If you currently have any "bad debt," the kind that isn't working for you, then focus on paying off high-interest debt such as credit cards. Stop making purchases unless you can afford the item and pay off the balances each month so that you don't accrue interest.

Examples of "bad debt" include:

- credit card debt
- personal loans
- payday loans

Reducing expenses begins with separating "need-based" expenses from "want-based" expenses. Wealthy people spend their money on "need-based" expenses, while reducing as much as possible their "want-based" expenses.

Examples of "need-based" expenses include:

- mortgage or rent payment
- car or lease payments
- all insurance payments
- groceries
- utilities

Examples of "want-based" expenses include:

- entertainment - dining out, daily coffee
- vacations

Start Investing as Soon as Possible with as Much as Possible

While many advisors recommend investing 10-15% of your income, why not increase that to 50%?

Wealthy people commonly invest well over half of their income. Another common trait of wealthy people is that they begin saving and investing money early in life.

But if you're like me, perhaps you didn't have all the pieces of the puzzle early in life. Does that mean that you and I have completely missed the train? Will we see only financial difficulties on our horizon? Fortunately, I can say "NO!"

When I became a widow almost 12 years ago, I felt a lot of fear about my financial situation. In my life up until that time, I had been skilled in saving, staying on budget, and being a wise steward of the money I had. But investment was not something that I felt confident about. I needed to become more financially savvy, so I began researching. My search left me feeling that there had to be better information available. Fortunately, I eventually found a group of people who were doing things with money that were not being widely taught.

The interesting thing was, their "money secrets" weren't actually secrets. In fact, the ultra-wealthy had been using these strategies for years. Families like the Rothschilds, the Rockefellers, and the

Kennedys used them, obviously with brilliant success. So, here's a thought: why don't the rest of us start doing the same thing?

The good news is that we can, and we don't have to start with a lot of money; we just have to get started. If we grow our money by hitting all the highs in the market, and not taking part in any of the lows, we will have an advantage we would not usually see in a typical 401K. If we grow our money tax-free, in a completely legal and IRS-sanctioned way, won't that be better than waiting to pay taxes during our retirement years when the tax rates will most likely have increased from where they are now? YES, it will!

Here are three places you can get started:

1. Private Reserve Account (PRA) – This is a customized accumulation tool, built in a way that meets specific criteria to achieve tax advantages.

- Tax-Free Growth - Similar to a Roth, after-tax dollars are used to fund a PRA. Therefore, growth is not taxable.
- Tax-Free Distributions – You can make tax-free withdrawals at any time, for any purpose, based on cash value.
- Tax-Free Benefit to Heirs – The death benefit component is never taxed upon payout to beneficiaries.

With a Private Reserve Account, you get the upside without the downside, because the cash value is tied to indexes of the market, but your investment is not actually in the market. Therefore, your cash can grow exponentially without ever losing value. You also get unlimited growth potential because, instead of making pennies in a bank account, CD, or money market, your account grows along with the market index. More importantly, you don't lose money when the market drops because these accounts are not directly in the market. Access to tax-free withdrawals from your Private Reserve Account makes this the perfect vehicle for college savings, retirement distributions, auto loan payoffs, and even as a mortgage alternative.

2. Lifetime Income - Knowing that you can never outlive your money is another great addition to your wealth strategy. You can achieve this by adding an annuity, or several, to your plan. An annuity is a long-term retirement savings product that can help protect you from outliving your money. It has the potential to grow tax-deferred, have death benefits to protect your beneficiary, and optional living benefits to protect your retirement income. You can choose how to fund your annuity, how interest is credited to it, and how you take payments from it.

3. Diversify Your Portfolio with Real Estate - Real Estate is widely recognized as a wealth accumulator. I'm happy to share that with as little as $40,000, you can become a real estate investor. Purchasing land along the path of projected growth is a great way to do this. The best part is, it is so simple!

a. Buy undeveloped commercial land in the path of growth.

b. Hold it for 7-10 years.

c. Sell it for exponentially more than you bought it... and then REPEAT!

The bottom line is, you can't print more land.

These and other strategies are the things I have implemented in my own Smart Money financial plan, and today I have the privilege of helping others do the same. Using a modern, savvy, and holistic approach to growing, investing, and protecting money is my passion. I have turned my pain into purpose, and today I empower my clients with financial strategies that will make them financially bulletproof.

I cherish my old photo albums, but I've also added some modern digital photo albums to my collection. These are filled with new experiences that my daughter, my son-in-law, my friends, and I are creating. New places, adventures, and trips are filling those pages, and there are many more to come.

There is still work to be done, and I'm on the same Money Path as my clients. But my goals are clearly defined, the best strategies are in place, and we're committed to the journey.

I invite you to jumpstart your wealth as well. It's as simple as booking a free, no-obligation Zoom call with me. I would like to learn about you and your goals, and then together we can create a plan that will help you achieve them. You can also find me and connect with me on LinkedIn and/or go to www.AnnaFelix.com/jumpstart to learn more, watch my video, and connect!

Don't think that if you are already working with an advisor, or two or three, that we can't work together. Nothing could be further from the truth. If your advisor hasn't mentioned these strategies, most likely they can't offer them or don't know about them.

Working with me doesn't have to affect your established relationship. We can implement these things in addition to what you're already doing. Reach out, let's have a conversation!

About the Author

Anna Felix

Anna is a California native and Smart Money Strategist. When she became a widow in 2010, she felt the need to become more financially savvy. Her search left her feeling that there had to be better information available. She decided to turn her pain into purpose, and today she empowers her clients with strategies for managing financial accounts, investments, insurance, beneficiaries, and anything else that will make them financially bulletproof.

Jumpstart
Your Business
Chapters

Jumpstart Your Business

3 Areas to Improve to Scale and Profit

By Katrina Sawa

After the pandemic hit, business was done differently.

The question is: Did you change with it?

If not, now is the time to change what you're doing to achieve greater success.

For me, the pandemic allowed me to make more money—more profit, really. I didn't spend a lot of money on traveling around the country to live events, on flights, hotels, etc., and instead I attended more virtual events, so most of my increase was actually having less in expenses. That's a great way to make more money of course, but let's face it, if we're not investing in ourselves and our businesses with professional- and self-development and mentorship, then we'll remain stagnant, or worse, we'll go out of business.

Improving and developing a few areas in your business could prove very lucrative, but you must get serious about growing and scaling your business and stay committed to doing it consistently.

Just imagine... It's three, two, or even just one year from now, and you have a consistent money-making business. That business is providing everything you need for your family, and you're not killing yourself working 24/7 to have it, either. In fact, you're working your ideal hours, helping your ideal clients and customers.

This can be your future if you do what it takes right now to achieve it. If you're an entrepreneur now, or if you want to be one, this chapter will share the main areas on which you will need to focus to get what you want and to go where you want.

I've owned my business since 2002, and all my prior jobs involved some sort of sales or marketing. It was my major in college. I've held various marketing and sales positions at many different companies. I've even sold door-to-door! I know what it takes to sell stuff and make money. I've been very good at it, and as the saying goes, I fully believe that "selling is serving." You must believe that what you offer is worth what you're charging (or more), and then you must pursue those who need it. Be assertive and do not back down. Be proud and loud about what you offer!

Let me share 3 areas for you to focus on and improve now, to help you scale and profit in this digital age.

Area #1: Foundational Strategies

What does your big vision look like?

I have found that many of my clients choose to work on goal planning and vision only once or twice a year. They set their Big Vision, and perhaps even design a Vision Board. Visioning can be a daily practice. Pairing it with your morning meditation is a surefire way to ensure success. As you make more and more money, your vision may change and grow, and you will do better in the world with that additional income.

What are you selling?

It is imperative for you to be clear on what specific products and services you offer through your business. What you're selling to your prospect, though, is the "transformation" that those products and services provide. What will be the outcome for them if or when they buy and use your products and services? If you are not 100% clear on what you are selling, or its price point, then you need to become clear. When you don't have absolute clarity on your offer, it is much harder to close the sale.

Whatever you offer, please make sure you charge "enough." Too many entrepreneurs don't charge enough because they don't believe they're worth it. Maybe you don't think you're worth a higher rate, because you haven't been "in the business long enough." Or perhaps you over-deliver by fixing additional problems and issues along with the ones for which you're being paid to fix—but you're not charging extra for the additional work. This will always be something to tweak and change as your confidence grows.

Confidence comes with clarity, and clarity comes with knowing exactly what you're selling and for how much. Knowing your price point will help you sell your wares with complete confidence because, if you've done your research and you know what you're worth, then you will stand tall and tell your potential new client your price without automatically giving a discount. Often, growing in confidence is just a matter of one or two clients paying you at a certain rate, and then you have proof. I tell my own clients to charge as much as they can say out loud without stuttering. When you can tell a potential client, "My coaching is $300 an hour," with a smile on your face and your chin up, then you're well on your way.

Do you look like the expert you are?

Your positioning affects everything these days—what you look like online, on your website, on social media, on Zoom, in public. Are you wondering why people may not be buying from you or reaching out to connect with you on your website or social media? I hate to say this, but maybe you simply don't look like an expert. I'm sorry to say this, and I don't want you to be offended, but I see it all the time: professionals try to get clients (particularly high-end clients), but they struggle because they just don't look the part.

Not that I look perfect every day either, frankly, but I exude a professional appearance on calls, networking events, speaking gigs, my live events and live videos, and especially on my website and my social media profiles! You must look the part. You must invest at least a bit of money to make yourself look pleasing and professional. That doesn't mean spending thousands of dollars for new branding or lifestyle photos. It just means that you have a professional appearance from the outside looking in. Your first impression is a big deal in this digital age.

How are you marketing and becoming visible?

When you're marketing, you need to be implementing more than just one or two strategies. In fact, I teach 20+ different marketing strategies in my workshops. You need to be open to trying new things, such as video marketing. More than half of my clients aren't excited about doing videos, but they work, and they do them anyway. If you hate social media and you think it's a waste of time, but you know your target market is hanging out there, then you must figure out how to be there to be visible to them. You can hire a Virtual Assistant to do the things you know you need to do but either don't like to do, don't know how to do, or don't want to do yourself.

Marketing is primarily about relationships and building community. You want to join some communities for networking and collaborations, and you may also decide to lead a community so YOU become the expert influencer. Find your way and what works for you and your business, your clients, and your personality, but don't avoid something just because you don't like it.

Embrace the right technology to make your life easier.

Technology can certainly help to save you time and keep you organized. Using technology to simplify your business could be as simple as tracking clients and potential clients in an Excel spreadsheet or implementing online banking. One thing that most business owners will need is an email marketing software to keep in touch with their customers. Another is having a shopping cart or payment processor... you can't be successful if you don't make money, and you want to make it easy for your clients to pay you. In addition, use Google Calendar and other scheduling software to keep you on task. I live by my calendar.

Sustain a positive money mindset with swift moneymaking decisions.

Try to be mindful of how you speak about money. Rather than focusing on scarcity and speaking about money negatively (e.g., "I can't afford that"), shift your mindset and say, "How CAN I afford this?" instead.

In addition, when evaluating monetary decisions, do it quickly and with your full attention. Don't let the decision linger, because your hesitancy is negative energy. Give the investment opportunity your full focus, feel it in your gut, and make the decision. I like to say, "Money follows speed!"

Area #2: Growth Strategies

How are you with creating systems in your business?

This step is a little more difficult for "control freaks." You think it's just easier for you to do everything yourself rather than take a moment to teach someone else how to do something in your business. It may take extra time in the short run, but in the long run, you'll be able to leave your business for weeks and still bring in revenue when you have the right systems and a reliable team. For example—if you spend too much time doing administrative tasks, bookkeeping, and follow-up by yourself, then you might be missing out on making more sales.

Systems aren't necessarily technologies; they are processes or strategies for how something will get done. You want procedures for each area of your business, whether it's marketing, follow-up, data entry, advertising, product delivery and shipping, etc. Without a plan, you're certainly wasting time and money. And having a team can mean hiring independent contractors for limited hours and minimal expense. Delegating allows for you to spend your time on the things that you do best.

Are you collaborating with others?

Affiliate marketing, joint ventures, and just plain doing things with others, collaborating, gets you in front of more people faster because you get in front of an entirely new audience. Growing your business means expanding your reach, your email list, and the number of followers on social media.

What next-level offerings will you have to grow?

In the growth stage of your business, it could be time to hold that 3-day event or retreat, perhaps write a book, start a podcast, and apply to speak on bigger stages. These are advanced strategies, though, so be careful doing them too early on.

Area #3: Scale Strategies

Don't settle for anything less than 100% personal happiness, love, and support.

This is the glue that holds everything together. If you are settling anywhere in your life, your business, your job, your relationship—this is toxic to your entrepreneurial energy. Only with the proper love and support in your personal life can you achieve full potential in your business. Things are going to happen in life: people go through hard times, illness, loss of family and friends, natural disasters, and poor decisions that result in terrible outcomes. But if your foundation is sound, if your support system is there, then you will get through. Protect your positive energy and try really hard to avoid negative people.

Are you seen as an influencer in your industry?

This is the stage where everyone sees you as such. They admire you and possibly even copy what you're doing because now you're the one to follow.

Elevate your systems, team, operations, and financials to those of a CEO.

It's time now to truly master the areas of running the business, bringing in the leads, and closing. If you're still living sale to sale, then you're not ready to scale just yet... keep working on the foundational aspects until you reach the stage where you have more freedom and no stress around money. It could take years to reach this stage. Some business owners never do. If you stick with it and stay consistent no matter what life throws at you, I know you can reach your big goals.

Follow these steps, and you, too, can create a business that continues to support your dreams and financially provides for you and your family. My business runs smoothly and pulls in money, whether I'm ill, on vacation, or working at the top of my game. This has been possible because I took the time to set up my business the right way from the start, and because I continue to invest in myself, my training, getting support from mentors, and hiring a team.

I want you to succeed as I have, so please go take my Jumpstart Your Biz Quiz now to find out what's missing in your business and where you want to focus this coming year! Go to www.JumpstartYourBizQuiz.com, then reach out and let's chat!

About the Author

Katrina Sawa

Katrina is the creator of The Jumpstart Your Business in 90 Days System, the International Speaker Network, and she's an International Best-Selling author of *Jumpstart Your New Business Now, Love Yourself Successful, and 18 other books.* She's been featured on the Oprah and Friends XMRadio Network, ABC, and TheCW. Katrina loves to inspire and educate entrepreneurs on how to create a consistent money-making business doing what they love.

Jumpstart Your Content Marketing

3 P's for Attracting More Clients

By Bonnie Chomica

Once upon a time, there was a young lady named Jessica who had just gotten a brand-new puppy, Maisie. As cute as she was, the puppy was chewing Jessica's Italian leather shoes, and Jessica was understandably upset. So, she looked on Google and came across a dog trainer's blog post about how to stop your puppy from chewing your shoes. While on the site, Jessica was pleased to find other blog posts with helpful puppy training information. This was great news because, as you can probably imagine, her puppy challenges were not just involving her shoes. It turned out that this dog trainer was in her local area and he had a puppy school, so she signed up right away for herself and Maisie.

That story is an example of content marketing at its most basic level. The dog trainer had written blog posts over a period of time around his ideal customer's challenges, in this case, puppy issues and how to solve them. His customer had discovered the posted information, found it useful in the moment, and it ultimately led to a sale for the dog trainer's puppy school. This example is for a local business, but it could easily have been an online product with puppy training videos or one-on-one video consultations that would reach a larger geographic audience.

The concept of content marketing is to create value-added content without the intent to promote or sell, but to position your company and brand as an authority in your industry or niche. Showcasing your expertise builds trust with your audience and can stimulate interest in your services or products.

Some of the major benefits of content marketing are: it is a long-term strategy that is low-cost or essentially free; it's powerful for SEO rankings (search engine optimization); and it builds your credibility while establishing that all-important "know, like, and trust" factor. Your free content also increases traffic to your website, creates brand awareness, attracts higher-quality leads, and facilitates email list-building strategies, to name just a few.

Consider your own online content-consuming habits. Typically, you search online because you have a question or a problem. The content you're seeking will have the answer to your question or a solution to your problem. Now, think about the content you need to create. What challenges does your ideal audience have for which you can provide the answer or the solution?

In most business cases, people are not ready to buy something at the very moment of their search, but they are doing research that can introduce them to your content, in which they will discover information that is valuable to them. Position yourself as the expert and authority in the industry or niche they're investigating, and you'll start building trust, sharing your knowledge and values, and cultivating a relationship with this person who has found your free content.

In Jessica's story, she had a problem, searched for a solution, and found the dog trainer's blog on his website. She was not aiming to purchase something; she was simply seeking information on how to stop Maisie from chewing her shoes. But the dog trainer's valuable content convinced her to buy a spot in his puppy school. You can bet that Jessica will sign up for the trainer's newsletter or follow him on social media because she already knows his information to be valuable. If she knows other people with puppies, now or in the future, there is a good chance that she will recommend people to follow him, or to sign up, or to check out the dog trainer's info.

I've mentioned blogs, which are one of the most powerful content marketing tactics because the posts sit on your website and are easily accessible, shareable, and considered "tops" in the SEO world. However, there are many other options: text, video, audio, and graphics. Most people think of social media, which can include all those elements, when they are looking at content creation. But email marketing is an essential tactic for content strategies: think e-newsletters, free mini-courses, and list-building activities. Lead magnets and downloadables like checklists and eBooks also show great value. Live streaming or recorded videos and podcasts are much more prevalent these days, as are speaking engagements. Yes, in-person live stages are lucrative, but with the evolution of online summits and other Zoom-related shows, you can get massive visibility in the online world. Speaking is a huge credibility builder, and an opportunity for people to experience you.

Like learning an instrument or another language, content marketing takes commitment and consistency to get results. You can't just start a blog post and stop writing three months later, or plan to do a series of Facebook Lives and then fizzle out, or start and stop an eNewsletter. You'll stop being visible, diminish your credibility, and lose your audience, who you have fought so hard to attract and nurture. Creating content can keep you top of mind for followers and potential clients. If you don't commit, no one will see you, get to know you, or eventually buy from you.

I'm certainly guilty of being a random or sporadic content creator in the past. But once I committed to working on content strategy, I developed a plan and a process, and it all became so much easier. I keep accountable to myself and my audience, which results in more engagement, more conversations, larger event registration numbers, and an increasing client list!

What is my approach, and how do I help my coaching clients to work on the 3 P's principal?

The 3 P's are Plan, Produce, and Promote. Let's look at each one.

1. Plan

Consistency takes planning. Think of yourself as a publishing company or a broadcast company. Those people have things planned out months in advance, often longer. Start off by planning a few weeks into the future and create your own rhythm.

As with any marketing initiative, start by knowing who you're talking to. Who is your ideal client, what are they struggling with, and how can you position yourself as someone who knows the solution? As you plan, keep a library of different topics that you can work on tomorrow or in the future.

What is the intent of your content? Is the purpose to educate, entertain, or enlighten? Remember, you're not trying to sell here. But you can lead them to further explore your online assets, like your website, an event, a video, etc. Always position yourself as an authority.

How you deliver your content is an important decision, because it has to be doable, repeatable, and effective. If you don't enjoy writing, a blog may not be the best tactic. Try video instead. If you don't fancy being on camera, a voice-only podcast may be your lane. Do you have creative design skills? Use infographics and other visual media.

You now have a target audience, a message, and a delivery platform. How often do you deliver your content? Start by setting achievable goals, creating a process, and committing to a regular schedule. If you want to write a weekly blog post but can't keep it up, start with a monthly post, then increase to a biweekly post, then move to weekly.

The last tool in the planning stage is some kind of content calendar. I have an effective spreadsheet Content Planner Tool I created, but you can also use online apps like Trello or Evernote. Even a poster with sticky notes will work, if you commit to using it.

There's that word again–commit! Do you see a theme here?

2. Produce

Once you know where you're headed with a topic, it's time to actually produce or create said content. Sometimes research is required for stats or validation. I find it valuable to create an outline or draft of what I'm creating, then finalize my writing or recording. If you're posting on multiple platforms, you may have to adjust the structure to be shorter or longer, create different graphic sizes, and adjust your call-to-action to best fit each platform.

A call-to-action is important because that's how you lead your audience where you want them to go next. It's not always a "Buy Now" statement. It can take them to other free content, or to sign up for an event or a free course, or to other content like a previous and related blog post. You may offer a free discovery call or a free quote option for potential clients. People want to be led. You are the leader with a logical and easy call-to-action.

To make your topic ideas easier to come up with, create and reuse evergreen content (something that's not time-sensitive). For example, I used to have a blog post that explained what you should do to promote your participation at a trade show. I would repost that blog article three times a year during heavy trade show seasons, and I didn't have to change anything.

It wasn't specific to a particular event, but I could repurpose that evergreen content because it wasn't time-sensitive.

Repurposing content is another easy way to be efficient and extend your content without always having to start from scratch. Years ago, I did a 45-minute speech about writing tips to attract clients. Then, I turned that speech into an eBook, which I still use for a lead magnet to this day. I created several blog posts from that content and hosted my own webinar as a list-building exercise. Many of my social media posts also repurposed that original speech content. All that repurposing happened on the fly over several years, but now I know better and I can actually plan what I will repurpose in the future—and how.

3. Promote

As you create your content, you must put it into action. A blog post, as an example, won't be seen by anybody unless you share it via email or social media. A Live Stream needs to be promoted ahead of time, to get people to your live show. There are often technical steps required, or tech nuances for different platforms.

By using different platforms, you can get in front of more people, often different people, and your connections can help share your posts and wisdom. Use groups, forums, and memberships, and even referral, affiliate, and power partners to share your content. You can reciprocate by sharing theirs, if their audience is similar. Consequently, you will build deeper relationships, opening the doors to greater opportunities.

Certain content (like blog posts) is great to share in emails or in chat messages to prospects, to provide value and share your knowledge without being salesy. You're sharing free, helpful information that positions you as an expert, and will be appreciated by the recipient.

Your Best Stuff

Your free content should also be your best content. Just because you're giving it away for free doesn't mean it should be unprofessional or poor quality. When someone looks at your free material, they should think, "Wow! If she's giving this to me for free, imagine what I will get if I pay for her services!" That's the approach you want to take with your content.

Content Marketing is your road to greater exposure to showcase your expertise to attract more clients. With one-on-one or group coaching, I can be your guide and advisor for planning your goals, your messaging, and all the moving parts of your content strategy, so you can move out of invisible mode and make more money.

To help you get started, I want to gift you my Content Marketing Toolkit!

You'll have access to my 9 Client-Attraction Writing Tips eBook and the Content Planner Tool, which I mentioned in this chapter, a list of 50 subject lines to help you increase open rates for your email, and an opportunity to do a Free Prosperity Call with me one-on-one. All are excellent tools for building a strong content marketing foundation. Go get your tools online at www.BonnieChomica.com/jumpstart.

About the Author

Bonnie Chomica

As The Content Creation Mentor, Bonnie Chomica guides her solopreneur clients to create and implement an effective content marketing strategy so they can showcase their expertise and be seen by more prospects. She takes them from producing sporadic content to consistently creating engaging and interesting content, so they can make more money by becoming the sought-after authorities in their niche. As their guide and advisor, cheerleading and handholding are included.

Jumpstart Your Publicity

6 Ways to Grow Your Visibility

By Lynette Hoy

I was eight years old, and after many years of growing in the automobile industry, my dad finally reached his goal of starting his own car dealership in Reno, Nevada. He built it from the ground up. He shared some of his struggles with me on the way, teaching me by example what it was to grow and become an entrepreneur. I could not have been prouder even though, as a kiddo, I did not understand everything about growing a business.

In those early days, I used to go to work with him, and he would set me up with my own "desk" (an upside-down cardboard box), and I was on my way! I had my play phone, and his secretary would bring me papers to "file." It was my job to make Dad's appointments, too. Even though it was just pretend, I remember feeling like I was involved and helping him! It was his perseverance and tenacity that I loved to watch. I was in awe and wanted to have my own business when I grew up. I watched him fall and get back up again. I saw him cry and throw things. He made many mistakes and never gave up. It scared me when he got angry, but the way he recovered and kept going was magical, and I lean into that memory to this day when things get rough.

Over the last few decades of growing my career, I have known great struggle, and I have become great friends with winning too! It is struggle that has been my best teacher. I know what it is to be at the bottom: it is what has fired me up to succeed. And now I want to share how I help others succeed. But first, let's dream a little.

Just imagine... for years now, you have been getting phone calls from journalists asking for quotes to add to their articles, and television producers are calling you to be a guest on the network evening news and daytime talk shows. Industry expert bloggers are reaching out to you and want you to be a guest blogger for them, and you get an average of two podcast guest requests a week. Then there are the frequent requests to be a guest on video television programs worldwide, and the list goes on. You are in the media spotlight!

Now, if the thought of this kind of exposure terrifies you, then it's likely you will NOT imagine yourself going after the media spotlight! Or, perhaps you simply don't see yourself putting in the energy to get there.

But what if you were *100% prepared and confident* for these moments and you *weren't* scared?

And here's the best part: you have grown your business to the point where you have a PR specialist that handles all the bookings for you. Your job is to just show up and shine and continue on your path to becoming a multiple-six-figure, then seven-figure earner!

Your business is quite successful, with a plethora of warm leads consistently flowing in because you have been building "know, like, and trust" to an audience of millions. You are seen and heard, and you hold the respect of people you don't even know. Yessss! You are leading the life of your dreams and helping others fulfill theirs. Inspiring others gets you out of bed in the morning, and you no longer dread the alarm clock. You got this!

However, right now, there are no interviews and no spotlights.

Perhaps you are interviewed on a podcast once a month, but that is not generating any leads for your business. You are envious of others who are consistently growing with media attention, and frustration mounts because you don't know where to start. It is in their feed on LinkedIn, the last interview they had. It is on other social platforms, too, with many congratulations, and even the interviewer pops into the comments to exclaim what a great interviewee they were. You Google them, and the first two pages are full of links to interviews, the articles they have written, the Online Media Kit on their website, a Pressroom full of their media wins, and more. You have been running your business on referrals alone, not bringing in the projected profit.

How do you change this and become the go-to expert the media is clamoring for? I know it seems overwhelming, and I feel you! But there is a way to change it, and it's easy! I work with entrepreneurs every day who quickly learn how to move forward.

You can change that trajectory starting right now.

It starts with the right mindset. You are frozen when you have no idea where to begin, and your Google searches on how to get media attention are confusing and overwhelming. The thought process around scarcity dictates that there is no way you will ever accomplish this dream. It is time to shift to an abundance mindset from preparation and mentoring. It provides the confidence to take the next step in increasing the visibility to get interviewed and gain publicity that grows credibility and, ultimately, profitability. That abundance mindset says there are more reporters, producers, and podcast hosts than you could ever serve!

I have helped thousands of entrepreneurs and small businesses grow into multiple-six-figure businesses by leveraging publicity to grow their businesses. You can do this too, but it requires you to become visible in the marketplace you serve, so when the media (that person who wants to interview you) searches your name, they see you are the credible expert they are looking for. This is called developing your visibility platform, which I liken to growing a garden: you prepare the soil, plant the seeds, and soon it becomes so bountiful the media can't ignore it! I see daily when that "just imagine" exercise becomes a reality.

What to do starting now:

1. **Give yourself a social media and website audit.** Does your LinkedIn profile position you as the expert you are? Do you have a professional headshot (not the same one as your personal profile on Facebook, where you are holding your poodle with sunglasses on)? Also, make sure you have a cover image that reflects your business and branding, and a LinkedIn business page. (Just Google how to do it.) Check your other social media platforms to ensure your branding is consistent on business pages. AND be sure you

are posting at least five days a week on social media—but seven is ideal. Remember, you are establishing a presence, and when the media checks your social channels, you want a string of recent and consistent activity. And your website: is it current and relevant? Are you following the right protocol to ensure you are getting consistent visitors who stay and experience you? Make sure you have Google Analytics set up for your website and monitor it weekly. If you have not heard of Donald Miller, he is a master of the website audit. Buy his book: *Building a StoryBrand: Clarify Your Message So Customers Will Listen*, on Amazon.

2. **Start writing.** Please make sure you post on your blog (on your website) every week, post an article on LinkedIn every week (don't make it complicated, focus on 300 words), and write for another user-generated platform like Medium.com. Remember, you are building that visibility garden by being seen online. When you get to the point where you are pitching the media and selling them your story and why you should be their go-to expert, you must have an online presence. If they like your pitch, they are going to research you before reaching out. If you are inconsistent in your branding and there are no articles out there that establish you as an expert, they will move on.

3. **Become a guest blogger** on free and paid platforms that offer the best reach, like Medium.com for example, and find someone in your industry who is not your direct competition and post on each other's blogs (from your website) to provide backlinks for each other. This is one of the best ways to increase your Search Engine Optimization (SEO). While you're at it, aim to become a regular contributor for a publication that has your ideal client as the audience. (This is one of my biggest recommendations.)

Go for low-hanging fruit to get publicity sooner than later.

4. **Get interviewed on podcasts**. Create a media one-sheet and a one-minute introduction, then post it on platforms including Podmatch.com, PodcastGuests.com, and matchmaker.fm. If you need help to create a media one-sheet and a one-minute recorded pitch (introduction), I am here to help. The one-minute pitch is something you record on Zoom, and provide the mp4 as part of the profile you build out on the podcast platforms. I will walk you through the process. In the special downloads page I created for you, I will even share my own one-sheet and one-minute introduction for you to use as a template. If you package yourself correctly, your chances of consistently getting interviewed are huge.

5. **Join Help A Reporter Out**, or HARO, a platform where you become the source for reporters. Growing yourself as a go-to expert for the media is an ongoing task and it can be daunting, but so worth it! Once you register, they send you three emails a day (yes, that is a lot, I know) with queries from reporters looking to interview YOU or quote you in their articles. It's wonderful because you have more than just one opportunity a day to find a query to which you can respond to add value and make a reporter's job easier.

6. **Stream live with videos on social media.** This is something anyone can do today, for free. What you share should apply to your audience, position you as an expert, and present a clear and easy call-to-action. Shorter videos are best, up to two minutes. If you are doing a live training or interview show, keep it to 20 minutes. Don't get hung up on being perfect. If you have good lighting, a good camera, and a background that is clean and professional, you are good to go. Make sure you look directly into the camera. Many of my clients find video to be an amazing way to grow credibility with the media, as it shows you know how to show up virtually and are well spoken. Event professionals also look at your videos to see how you show up and deliver; even though it is not a "speaking engagement," they are still investigating how you present with different messaging.

Whether you're a business owner or you work in an organization and want more publicity coverage, I can help you.

Where do you begin? How can you become the go-to expert the media wants to interview?

First, we must get you confident about your speaking topic or message. Getting clarity on your soundbites, those short pieces of content that the media loves to hear, helps tremendously with increasing your confidence.

Then it's time to position you online with more credibility and a "WOW" online presence—a beautiful and professional-looking website, social profiles, etc. If you do not have an online presence, your chances for media pickup are close to zero.

Next, we'll create the ongoing plan for how you'll consistently implement this long-term business growth and visibility strategy. That includes building out your signature Online Media Kit that is professional and designed for the media to fall in love with you. We will lay out your Pressroom and set you up for success, even if you don't have any media coverage yet. You will also learn how to research and build relationships with the media, create a pitch and a press release, and build relationships with the *right media.*

Having support through this entire process not only helps with accountability and consistency, but it also provides encouragement, ideas, and leverage.

You can hire an expensive public relations agency, or you can work with a boutique firm like mine. You can either work one-on-one with me to do the work yourself, or I can do it for you.

I want to offer you the opportunity to schedule a complimentary discovery call with me, plus give you access to everything I have mentioned in this chapter, including a free publicity checklist that gives you a lot of resources and websites to get this process going on your own. I have created a special page on my website just for you, with a video so you can also get to know me and why I'm so passionate about helping entrepreneurs jumpstart their publicity. Plus, you'll find a link to access my Facebook group, where I post videos weekly!
Go to www.FiretalkerPR.com/jumpstart today, and let's get you some publicity this month!

Here's to reaching those revenue goals sooner than later and living the life of your dreams!

About the Author

Lynette Hoy

Since 1994, publicity expert Lynette Hoy has practiced public relations in different capacities, including founding Firetalker PR. She has worked with organizations like the National Institutes of Health and the American Cancer Society to put their products, services, and events on the map, and turned C-suite executives into speakers and thought leaders featured in major media. A fiery idea generator, Lynette's VIP mentoring program and other services increase the bottom line!

Jumpstart Your Soul Purpose

5 Ways to Prosper Using Your Genius

By Grace Mosgeller

Everyone has a soul, but few take time to get to know it. For women entrepreneurs who are here to expand the impact of their service or message and create true wealth doing it, not knowing the purpose of your soul, its unique gifts, and its personality is a huge mistake.

It's a huge mistake because without connecting with this hidden inner power, you may find success and reach your goals, but you'll end up exhausted, burned out, and no matter what you do, you'll continue to feel an internal dissatisfaction or emptiness that nothing you've ever won or achieved can fill.

Or, you'll find yourself in a repeating pattern of hustle that never makes "enough" progress. You may feel like a fish trying to climb a tree, yet you're determined to pull up your bootstraps and continue "the push" to succeed and climb it anyhow.

When you know your soul purpose, your energy vibration expands to match your business and your big money goals. A deep, unstoppable passion stirs from within you that becomes a driving force and "pulls" you to create true wealth. True wealth is financial abundance, plus an abundance of friends, family, followers, as well as physical, mental, and emotional health and well-being.

You'll experience a deep, unwavering belief in yourself, in your personal value, and an unshakable knowing of how to live and create your best life during each moment. You'll have freed and released yourself from the hustle of overthinking, over-doing, overwhelm, and procrastination, and become an irresistible magnet instead.

The authentic connection you'll have with your audience and family will lead to increased productivity, team synergy, and profitability. People will beg to hire you, partner with you, and work for you.

If you want results like that, I invite you to jumpstart your soul purpose by writing down at least 5 qualities you recognize within yourself as you read on. As you do, you can begin to self-validate who your authentic self truly is.

What is the purpose of your soul?

The purpose of your soul is to experience joy and unconditional love. HOW you express love and experience joy is determined by the unique combination of soul personalities and their qualities you have been given.

There are 5 base soul personalities that everyone has in different quantities which, together with deeper spiritual centers in your energy system, create the unique YOU.

When you are awake and aware, you focus your business to create love and wholeness, not only to make money and survive.

When you are not aware of who you are, you unconsciously live hidden behind a mask that disconnects you from yourself and others. The mask appears as ego-driven beliefs, behaviors, and habits that may keep you safe and get you what you "think" you want, but this way of living eventually wears you out, and your money story never feels truly good enough or fulfilling.

Before I discovered my soul's purpose and personalities, I never would have considered myself a strong leader or found the fearlessness to show others how to find their own authentic presence and escalate personal power. I never would have embraced the wacky, super-creative, and brilliant part of myself as a gift, rather than an affliction I needed to hide. I grew into adulthood staying true to my family's overachieving vision of being successful, ignoring my very different but equally successful nature. I eventually became so worn out that I ended up with adrenal fatigue that escalated into chronic fatigue. I couldn't surpass the "get by" level of income and reach my big-money goals, no matter what proven system I used or what expensive coach I hired. The more I aligned with my authentic self, the less fatigued I became, and my money story began expanding beyond the survival ceiling. I am now free of those energy-robbing conditions.

So, what are the 5 personal qualities of your soul?

1. Charismatic Leader
2. Knowledgeable Achiever
3. Creative Idealist
4. Team Player
5. Emotional Intelligent Specialist

Leaders have big energy, and they have access to all 5 of the soul qualities so that they can understand, gain trust, and build rapport with those they lead. As a leader in your natural state, you inspire trust, action, and loyalty, maybe as a teacher, an advocate, or as someone fighting for a cause or a group of people you represent.

Leaders have the double-edged gift of being able to scare or charm the skin off a snake, depending upon the situation. They hate to be told what to do, rarely ask for help, are slow to trust and won't follow anyone they don't respect. When they walk into a room, they immediately scan for who's in charge and assess where they fit in the pecking order. They LOVE TO WIN, almost at any cost, depending upon their individual moral code.

Leaders have a HUGE deep-feeling heart that is the driving force behind their leadership, but they hardly ever show it because if they did, they might appear weak or be taken advantage of. When in "battle" they often appear cold and commanding because they have to make the hard decisions and inspire their followers to jump into battle with them. Their huge sensitive hearts make them super-intuitive and more sensitive than they want others to know about. When they are scared or stressed, they can bully, and when overwhelmed, exhausted, or things don't go their way, they may slip into a "poor me" state where they either wallow in self-pity or push through, depending upon their secondary soul personality quality. They tend to be selfish and can have unconscious narcissistic tendencies.

When I recognized leadership personality traits in myself and accepted them, two life-changing awareness's happened: I gave myself permission to step up as a stronger, more understanding and compassionate leader and better understood poor behaviors in myself and my parents that I had judged and punished so harshly. With deeper self-reflection, I lifted blocks to productivity and big-money goals with forgiveness and completeness. I would never have been ready to do without this awareness.

If you have a strong achiever personality, you love systems and organization, and become a master of your craft. You rarely change jobs, let alone careers. You love structure, repetition, details, and rules. Your heart loves to serve others by organizing chaos or bringing structure and systems to wild and crazy new innovations so they can be brought into reality. You are grounded, live in the black and white real world, and it's easy for you to amass great financial wealth.

A telling sign you are an achiever is that when someone doesn't cross their "t's" or dot their "i's" it drives you crazy. Because you love rules, you likely have a strong inner critic to police them and have superior standards that rank close to perfection. When you get stressed, overwhelmed, or burned out, you lock down, become overly anal about rules, and/or become very controlling. You may want to fall into a "poor me" escape pattern, but the strong rule-keeper inside of you will command you to pull up your boots and carry on. Accountants, lawyers, physicians, and government servants who love their jobs and excel easily in them possess a huge dose of the achiever soul quality.

Creative idealist soul personalities love the world by sharing their super-creative, super-intelligent, super-imaginative ideas, innovations, and art. They can be natural visionaries who serve the world as pioneers or inventors of new ways of seeing, being, or doing the world. Or, they can create timeless works of art, discover new science, or do things more effectively in sci-fi ways. They are the Einsteins, Steve Jobs, and the Georgia O'keefs of the world.

They appear to be nerdy and slightly crazy because they see the world from a different perspective. In fact, they often appear to be stupid because when they hear or see one word or one concept, their brains immediately satellite out into the cosmos and find 15 ways to describe the one concept—but have trouble deciding which stream of thought to share. Because they can entertain themselves and get lost in space easily, they can be disconnected from people, even though they care deeply about them. Their brilliant ideas and innovations need to partner with an understanding achiever to give them structure and focus and bring their ideas to reality. The achiever soul needs the creative soul to help them expand and see beyond the limits of their reality so they can achieve the growth and impact of their mastery.

When creatives get stressed or scared, they leave their bodies and become ungrounded. They tend to experience unreasonable anxiety, especially when they start a new project. They typically avoid conflict and instead of showing their anger, they'll check out mentally or just leave.

If you have a strong team player soul personality, you are naturally wired to serve by giving your heart and soul in loyal support of a leader, a tribe, or a cause you care about, almost to a fault. You are a natural networker and connector. When you become stressed, you will give and do more. As a prideful over-giver, you can easily be taken advantage of and find yourself secretly resentful of those you love and support. You aren't wired to show your anger until the day you've had enough.

Emotional intelligence specialists are deep feelers whose purpose in life is to love unconditionally, accept mistakes and flaws, rinse, and repeat. They are extremely sensitive, loving, and very intuitive or psychic. They shy away from large groups and leading others, but when they feel safe, they have a glow of love they share freely. When overwhelmed or stressed, they break down into a teary-eyed, disempowered "poor me" state. Like the team player, they rarely get angry, because they are wired to understand and accept. They typically have fulfilling careers taking care of young children and babies, plants, or animals.

Please note that every charismatic leader has a deep-feeling emotionally intelligent heart within them which, when nurtured and awakened to their unique purpose, opens them up to a fearlessness that allows them to face any danger and move mountains to fulfill their purpose.

Self-Reflection Activity:

Review the awareness with which you identified in each soul category, then ask yourself:

- What new discoveries did you uncover?
- With which soul personalities do you identify?
- How will you embrace this awareness to jumpstart the soul behind your business?

You may have masked or hidden qualities that, when discovered and accepted, unleash your business and big-money-making genius.

That is why it saddens me to see:

- Smart corporate refugees who are used to making $20-$30K per month frustrated they aren't making that in their own businesses, even with lots of speaking gigs and enrollment conversations.

- Speakers who wish they could wow their audiences and captivate, connect with, and convert them into paying customers with their deepest authentic presence, but don't know how.

It saddens me because my guess is that you are likely experiencing a similar frustrating situation.

I know that, when you jumpstart your soul purpose and apply the principles of spirituality, you can stop hustling for "not enough" and start creating true wealth.

If you are serious about finding your true calling to grow your business and make big money, please schedule a free call with me. I love talking this through with people, and I have proven systems and questions to help you gain clarity. You can start by taking my Soul Purpose Assessment to identify your unique blend of soul qualities and begin to integrate what you learn into everything you do. Go to a special page on my website just for readers of this book, and gain access to your free assessment and additional information at www.GraceMosgeller.com/jumpstart.

Here's to living your best life sooner than later!

About the Author

Grace Mosgeller

Grace Mosgeller is a 25-year veteran of spiritual development and solopreneurship who is passionate about teaching soul-to-soul communication. She is an author, speaker, and communication coach-energy healer, because she knows firsthand how frustrating and limiting it feels when audiences don't connect or engage with you, or buy what you are selling—and how unbelievably impactful, pleasurable, and fulfilling it feels when they do.

Jumpstart Your Success

... In an Ever-Changing World

By Ivano Ongaro

Full disclosure: past success does not guarantee future success. This means that what worked to make your business successful last year (or yesterday) may not work today or tomorrow. This is because, over the last few years and to this day, our planet has witnessed many unprecedented changes, including:

- A global pandemic
- Behavioral and political changes that disrupt our society
- Extreme environmental events that impact billions of people
- Disruptions in the global supply chains

- Global recession
- International conflicts that threaten nuclear war
- New technologies that have transformed how we do everything

The survival of your business depends on your awareness of these unprecedented changes, how they will affect your life and your business, and what adjustments you can make to your life and your business to continue along your success journey.

I consider myself very fortunate. Having started life as the poorest immigrant kid on the block with poor but loving and strict parents, I've had a great life with a loving wife of 44 years and counting. I've had a successful career as a dentist in private practice, serving my community for 40 years. I've spent 12 years as an award-winning university professor, and 14 years as a brick-and-mortar business owner. My wife and I have three loving and successful children and four grandchildren. Life is good. For all this, I am grateful.

My good fortune was not an accident. My success was the consequence of learning valuable lessons from my parents. I carefully analyzed the economic and social environment in which I operated, and my good decisions outnumbered my poor ones. My attitude of striving for excellence in all my endeavours drove me to educate myself in matters that my parents did not teach me, and which I hadn't learned in school and college. Researching, learning, and applying the right information led me to make decisions that resulted in good profits in my businesses and excellent capital gains over the years. These decisions also resulted in my happy marriage and a wholly satisfying life.

Let's examine 8 of the aforementioned events and determine how they can affect your success and with what measures you might counter the negative effects of these events.

1. **The Global Pandemic** - COVID-19 had a devastating global impact on societies. Attempts to limit the damage of the spreading illness through lockdowns disrupted the social lives of billions of people. Circumstances forced millions of small businesses to close, and many went out of business.

   We were fortunate; the government considered our business to be an essential service because we sold building materials, and we were allowed to stay open. Like all other businesses that continued to operate, we had to comply to rigorous standards with physical barriers, hygiene and disinfection protocols, and all employees had to comply with social distancing regulations and wearing of masks. We were fortunate that, throughout the Covid restriction period, none of our employees got sick.

The financial consequences to our business were significant, particularly in the first year of the lockdowns. This was when the fear and uncertainty of customers prevented workers from coming into their homes for fear of catching the disease. We persevered, and now we are recovering financially.

2. **Changes in Human Behavior** - Truth and trust are intimately related, and when truth erodes, so does trust—and when trust erodes, customers won't purchase. Amplified by social media, a disturbing trend has emerged: the explosion of misinformation and outright falsehood. As a seller or provider of goods or services, the atmosphere of general mistrust will impact your ability to sell your services. Understanding this trend will help you manage this challenge.

   Referrals, which have been the mainstay of most businesses and professions for centuries, will continue to be a major source of new business for you, and there are tools that can expand your reach.

3. **Scientific Ignorance** - We live in a world that is governed by certain universal laws. Science is the study of understanding the laws that govern how the universe works. It is the understanding of these laws that has brought us electricity,

automobiles, modern medicine, and all manner of technologies that make our life so comfortable—there are too many to mention. Science is the source of intellectual freedom. Whether or not you believe in science, it's like gravity: it works universally regardless.

4. **Political Changes** - A disturbing movement that is growing in many countries around the world is the sentiment that Totalitarianism is a good thing. Humanity has struggled for millennia to get out from under the yolk of tyrants, despots, and kings. As a global citizen, you must do your part to maintain liberty and justice for all. No Totalitarian rule has demonstrated the benefits of our Western democracy.

5. **Extreme Environmental Events** - We have been bombarded by news of wildfires, devastating floods, destructive tropical storms, and ice storms. Collectively, these events have destroyed lives, homes, businesses, and infrastructure that will take years and immense amounts of capital to rebuild. These events have a tremendous impact on their own, but they are only a part of the collective economic and psychological impact on lives and economies.

6. **Disruptions in the Global Supply Chains** - No one anticipated the impact on global distribution caused by cyber-attacks on logistics companies,

Covid restrictions that shut down ports, factories, and shipping, and essential workers like mariners, port workers, and truck drivers getting sick and becoming unable to work and deliver goods. Global distribution was further disrupted when governments imposed restrictions on the movement of unvaccinated people and workers across borders. Shops and businesses that relied on these deliveries suffered delays, loss of revenue, and lost contracts, further worsening their financial position. Many had to furlough employees or shutter their stores, many permanently.

7. **Global Recession** - The accumulated destruction of financial wealth caused by the nearly simultaneous occurrence of the above calamities is staggering. Many other factors acting together caused the stock market to lose almost 20% of its value since 2021. Crypto currencies that were supposed to be disconnected from the stock market have lost as much as 60% or more of their value over the last year. The total loss of value to Bitcoin investors is over $600 Billion. Much wealth has vaporized during this time.

8. **New Technologies** - Technology is a double-edged sword. It is a constant evolution, and it will continue to transform almost everything we do.

   Elon Musk has single-handedly altered the face of

the automotive industry, which will significantly impact the petroleum industry.

Artificial Intelligence (AI), robotics, and Block-chain are more disruptive technologies that will change the way we carry out business. Robotics will replace physical labor, AI will replace intellectual labor, and once virtual currencies become mainstream, automatically tracking transactions and taxes, bookkeepers and other financial industry professionals will become obsolete.

Perhaps the most disruptive new technology of all is Fusion Energy. Billions of dollars have been invested in several candidates that are near break-even output energies. These Fusion Energy possibilities promise abundant low-cost energy. How will the millions of people currently employed in these industries earn a living?

We have examined a few of the most disruptive events that have happened (and are currently happening) that will undoubtedly have a significant impact on your present and future success. This list is not exhaustive, and many of these events are beyond your control but will affect you nonetheless. Many of these events have caused or contributed to the destruction of property, infrastructure, resources, wealth, and life. They affect the happiness and wellbeing of billions of people.

Anyone who is prepared to spend money on non-essentials will approach their purchase choices with a tighter wallet and greater scrutiny. Fewer people will open your emails or purchase your offers. They likely have other, more pressing financial concerns to manage.

These events present all of us with challenges and problems. The degree to which you can respond and adapt to these challenges and help others will determine whether you will survive or grow and thrive as a business.

Several factors are within your control, however. In my current coaching and consulting business, I help other entrepreneurs manage these factors so they can experience greater success and happiness.

As you can imagine, I look way beyond simply how you market your business to get clients. I take it a big step further and examine many areas, including environmental aspects, that also affect your business. A broad foundation makes for a robust building that can withstand many environmental stresses; this is true for your business.

Here are a few things to consider when focusing on your journey to success:

1. Intellectual Freedom is the only true freedom. You can control your own thoughts and behaviours.
    - Choose to stay on the path of integrity in your

daily interactions with family, friends, and customers.

- Act with truth and honesty towards everyone. Avoid expediency, and you will gain trust and new business.
- Strengthen associations with like-minded people who are focused on improving life for everyone.
- Be kind in your thoughts, words, and actions towards those who are most opposed to your way of thinking.

2. Trust yourself and have faith that you will make the best decisions.
3. Cultivate an optimistic attitude. A positive attitude paves the way for positive results. Things will improve.
4. Strive for a better world. Identify problems that others are not seeing and solve them.
5. Look for possibilities and find the opportunities to help and support others; this will lead to greater income.
6. Innovate: find new and better ways to do what we are already doing.
7. Be a shining beacon of hope. Your words and examples will encourage those who are struggling.

8. Listen to your customers. What are their current needs or wants? Satisfy those needs and wants, and you will thrive.

9. Be a catalyst of change. Change is happening; be part of it, and you can influence through your creativity for a better outcome.

10. Be grateful. Even with all the destructive events we've seen, we are living in a time of unprecedented wealth and prosperity. Gratitude releases neural transmitters that make us feel happy and energized and allow us to cultivate better relationships with others.

11. Aspire to make life better for others through contribution and collaboration.

12. The safest possessions are those that are stored inside your brain. No one can take them away from you. You can share your knowledge or sell it as you choose. Your greatest wealth is your repertoire of thoughts, dreams, and plans. They will make you wealthy. Remember Napoleon Hill's book, Think and Grow Rich.

13. Invest in yourself. Cultivate a lifelong desire to learn new things. Invest in your intellectual wealth first. Good fortune happens when opportunity meets preparedness.

14. You must take action! Each step, however small, will move you closer to your goals and dreams.

If any of these seem like good next steps for you to work on, I'd love to have a conversation with you to determine how I can point you in the right direction or impart any advice that might assist you. Please go to my website to get in touch, schedule a call, and access my free report, "Three Barriers to Wealth and How to Overcome Them," online at www.IvanoOngaro.com/jumpstart.

I would like to close this with a quote by Reinhold Niebuhr that I heard in my youth, embraced, and which has served me well for decades:

"God grant me the serenity to accept the things I cannot change, courage to change the things that I can, and the wisdom to know the difference."

About the Author

Ivano Ongaro, B.Sc., D.D.D. (dist.), M.Sc.

Ivano is an entrepreneur, published author, and artist. Now retired from a successful 40-year dentistry career and a 12-year career as an award-winning educator and mentor, he is currently partner in Edmonton Flooring in Canada. As the founder of the Success Academy, he shares his wisdom and broad experience in business, entrepreneurship, and the pursuit of excellence through courses and coaching on personal success and building wealth.

Jumpstart Your Team

6 Keys to Hiring Your Dream Team

By Mel Carr

Like most business owners, you probably want more profit, right? I know, me too.

More profit means you can start living the life you love. You'll have more time for family, vacations, self-care, and/or expanding and investing in other things!

One way to make more profit is by hiring and expanding your team. *(This is true even if you think you can't afford it yet.)* Expanding your team beyond yourself is essential to building a successful, more profitable business. It's the moment in your business when you finally take it seriously and realize you will not get where you want to go all on your own.

Your team can consist of employees and staff, but it can also include independent contractors. It can include consulting with mentors or coaches, and perhaps even hiring an accountant or an attorney. Your team is everyone who plays a part in moving your business forward.

In this chapter, I'm going to talk about building your main support team with independent contractors. Hiring a Virtual Assistant, better known as a VA, can be one of the best decisions you ever make for your business. A VA can provide a wide range of services, from administrative support to marketing, tech support, and social media management.

As the owner of a successful virtual assistant company, I'm here to tell you that hiring "the right" virtual assistant (or two or three) can be invaluable. Your VA can take on a variety of tasks, freeing up your time so you can focus on the marketing and sales activities it takes to grow your business.

But with so many choices out there, how do you know which virtual assistant is right for you?

When looking to hire your first virtual assistant, there are 6 key things to keep in mind.

1. It's essential to find someone who is a good fit for your business and your personality.
2. You'll need to decide what tasks you want your VA to handle. Define the tasks you need help with.

Before you start your search for a virtual assistant, take some time to sit down and think about all the tasks you need help with daily or weekly. This could include things like social media management. But remember to specify: is it the content creation you need help with, the writing and image creation, or just the posting? Or do you need help in all those categories, plus the engaging with others online? There is more than ONE task when it comes to social media. What about handling customer service, scheduling appointments, data entry, updating your website, posting on your blog, or even just general administrative work? I've gone into depth on a few of the most common tasks I see business owners delegating below. Having a clear idea of the tasks you need help with makes it easier to find a VA that is a good fit for your business. And remember, first you want to delegate the things that take up the most time in your day and/or the things you're not so good at. And you will certainly want to delegate those things which you dread doing.

3. Consider your prospective VA's skills and experience; not all virtual assistants are created equal! When you're searching for your perfect VA, be sure to look at their skills and experience to ensure they're a good fit for the tasks you need help with. For example, if you need help with

social media management, look for a VA with experience in that area.

4. Set up a trial period. Once you've found a few potential virtual assistants, set up a trial period to see how they work and if they're a good fit for your business. Make sure you set clear expectations, deadlines, and communication channels. This trial period could be anything from a few days to a couple of weeks—it just depends on what works best for you. During this time, please provide feedback to the VA so they can adjust their work to better suit your needs.

5. Ask for recommendations. If you're unsure where to start your search for a virtual assistant, ask your friends or business associates for recommendations. Chances are, someone you know has already hired a VA and they can point you in the right direction.

6. Utilize online resources. There are several great online resources that can help you find a qualified virtual assistant, such as job boards, directories like Fiverr, Upwork, 99Designs, and social media VA groups. Be sure to use these resources when searching for your perfect VA! *(Oh, and come see me, too, at Cloversy.com, I'll bet we can help!)*

Now, some people have a problem just getting past the point of figuring out what to delegate or even how to get started. Where do you find the time, right? You are already strapped for time. Well, just like anything else, if you want something to change, focus on it. Take the time to map out how you want to do it and figure out where you want to begin.

Here are some of the most common tasks you can delegate to a virtual assistant:

1. **Social media management:** Posting updates, responding to comments, monitoring analytics.

   As a business owner, you know social media is vital to building and maintaining a successful online presence. But between running your business and managing your personal life, finding the time to post updates, respond to comments, monitor analytics, and generate leads on all your social media platforms can be challenging. A virtual assistant can take care of your social media needs, freeing up your time to focus on other aspects of your business. From posting updates and responding to comments to monitoring analytics and generating leads, a virtual assistant can help you make the most of your social media presence.

2. **Email management:** Answering customer inquiries, setting up auto-responders, managing scheduling conflicts.

   Email is one of the most essential tools in the modern business world. It is a quick and easy way to communicate with customers, clients, and colleagues. However, email can also be a significant source of stress and anxiety. Sorting through a cluttered inbox, responding to customer inquiries, and managing scheduling conflicts can be time-consuming and overwhelming. Fortunately, a virtual assistant can take on these email-related tasks, freeing up your time to focus on other priorities. A virtual assistant can manage your inbox, draft and send email responses, and schedule email messages in advance. In addition, a virtual assistant can help you create auto-responders for common questions and set up email filters to prioritize particular messages. As a result, working with a virtual assistant can help you reduce email-related stress and optimize your productivity.

3. **Calendar management:** Booking appointments, setting up reminders, sending out invitations.

   A virtual assistant can be a great calendar manager, handling both the big-picture view and the day-to-day details. They can work with you to block off time for important projects, book appointments, and send out invitations as needed. They can also set up reminders for upcoming deadlines or events, ensuring that you're always on top of your schedule. In addition, a virtual assistant can help to resolve calendar conflicts, ensuring that your schedule is always manageable. As a result, a virtual assistant can be a valuable asset in keeping your calendar organized and streamlined.

4. **Data entry:** Entering information into databases, updating customer records, transcribing meeting notes.

   In today's business world, customer data is essential for keeping track of customer records and improving customer service. A virtual assistant can help with data entry in several ways. First, they can help to enter information into databases. This can include customer information, contact details, and any other relevant data. Second, they can help to update customer records. This can involve adding new customer data, updating existing data, or removing outdated information. Finally, a virtual assistant can transcribe meeting notes. This can be beneficial for businesses that need to keep track of meeting minutes or other essential details. Having accurate customer data is necessary for providing the best possible customer service.

5. **Research:** Conducting market research, gathering data on competitors, compiling industry reports.

   A virtual assistant can be a valuable asset when it comes to research. They can help you gather data on your competitors, compile industry reports, and even conduct market research. Plus, a virtual assistant can provide valuable insights and perspectives that you might not get on your own. Whether you're looking for information on a specific industry or market, or you need help to gather data for a report or presentation, a virtual assistant can save you time and hassle.

6. **Project management:** Creating project plans, assigning tasks to team members, following up on the progress of projects.

   Project management can be a complex and time-consuming task, especially for businesses with multiple ongoing projects. A virtual assistant can help relieve some of the burden by creating project plans, assigning tasks to team members, and following up on the progress of projects. By having a dedicated virtual assistant to handle project management, businesses can focus their attention on other areas. In addition, a virtual assistant can be a cost-effective solution for companies that do not have the need for a full-time project manager.

7. **Website and technology management:** Keeping your website up to date, free from spiders, and consistently adding new content to stay fresh is key.

   Website technology can be complicated, and the non-techy-minded business owner can become very frustrated with involvement in their website details. Some build it but forget about it, which I do not advise. You need to introduce new content monthly, if not weekly. You must do updates and fix links that become broken. Plus, you want to stay fresh and one step ahead of your competition. Your website is a great place to showcase what you do and how.

Delegating tasks to a virtual assistant is an excellent way for business owners to free up their time so they can focus on the tasks they enjoy and which grow their business. When creating a list of tasks to delegate, business owners should keep in mind the skills of their virtual assistant, the amount of time they will delegate, and which tasks they enjoy doing themselves. By considering these factors, business owners can delegate confidently and reap the benefits of having a virtual assistant on their team.

Another thing that goes hand-in-hand with increased profitability in your business is always looking for ways to improve efficiency and productivity.

One thing we do at my company is to set up standard operating procedures (SOPs). We use online software to manage the projects we're working on with clients and often the clients have access and they are involved in the process. Other times, clients want to be hands off. SOPs help you maintain efficiency and when you have to switch people on your team or train new team members, you have systems and processes for them to go by; you don't have to start from scratch.

The hiring process for a virtual assistant is like hiring any other employee. You want to make sure that the person you hire is qualified and capable of performing the tasks you need them to do. When interviewing potential candidates, be sure to ask about their experience, skills, and availability.

You should also create a list of tasks or jobs that you need to delegate to free up your time to grow your business. Be sure to give your virtual assistant clear instructions and deadlines for each task. By following these tips, you'll be well on your way to finding and hiring your first, second, or even third virtual assistant!

And if you would like to speak with me about what my team and I can help you with, **I've put together a special page on my website with a big list of 40+ tasks you could delegate, as well as a free video training on how to build and grow your team.** You can also have a virtual or in-person conversation with me! Visit www.Cloversy.com/jumpstart and get going today!

About the Author

Mel Carr

Mel Carr is the founder of Cloversy, a US-based Executive Virtual Assistant company that supports entrepreneurs who are looking to scale their businesses. She has a wealth of experience in helping business owners manage their time and priorities. Cloversy was created to provide high-quality support to entrepreneurs who want to grow their businesses without sacrificing their time or energy. Mel is passionate about helping business owners achieve their goals.

What's Next?

What did you think of the stories and expertise that our authors had to share?

Did you learn a few new things to take back to your life or work?

My hope is that you did learn a few things, or at least walk away with a fresh new way of thinking about some of our topics. If so, please go over to Amazon and leave us a review! Make sure you choose the "purple" colored *Jumpstart Your* _____ book as there are four others there.

Our authors have been hand-selected due to their level of expertise, genuine integrity, and overall skill level in their industry. If you enjoyed reading some of their stories or learning more about how they help their clients, please take the next step and reach out to those who spoke to you.

Most of the authors in this book speak to groups of all sizes, both in person and virtually. They also offer products, programs, events, and services that can support you in one or more areas of your life, health, or business / career.

I highly recommend that you take advantage of their special offers, additional downloads, and more when you visit each of the websites listed at the end of their chapters.

In addition, I've put together ONE page on my website where you can access all of the Jumpstart Author's websites and special offers, to make it easy for you to follow up. **Go to www.JumpstartBookAuthors.com** right now, before you forget who you wanted to connect with or find out more about. All authors from all Jumpstart books are on that page.

Thank you for reading this book, and I look forward to bringing you more Jumpstart Your _____ Authors in upcoming books, plus more training and teachings in my own books.

If you are an author who has something that YOU help people JUMPSTART and you would like to be considered as one of our next Jumpstart Authors, please go to www.JumpstartPublishing.net now and apply!

WHAT DO YOU HELP YOUR CLIENTS JUMPSTART?

In the *Jumpstart Your* _____ book series, YOU Fill in the Blank with the thing YOU do with YOUR clients for YOUR chapter, and become an author this year! Use this book as a MARKETING TOOL to get leads and grow your business.

Interested in becoming an author easily?

Get into a compilation book of 12-20 authors and write ONE chapter, but get huge exposure for you and your business, along with every author promoting it alongside you! Attract new clients and make more money after your prospects are introduced to you in this book.

Want to get more exposure, speaking gigs, or clients in the coming year? Become an author!

While it could take a while for you to write your own full book, it's relatively easy to get published in an anthology or compilation book by just writing one chapter. Everyone in the book promotes the books and sells them, so you get in front of a lot more people than you would with just your own book. PLUS... we do all the work! **Find out how this could benefit you here:**

www.JumpstartPublishing.net.

ABOUT KATRINA SAWA

CEO OF K. SAWA MARKETING INT'L INC., JUMPSTART PUBLISHING, AND THE INTERNATIONAL SPEAKER NETWORK

Katrina Sawa is known as the JumpStart Your Biz Coach because she literally kicks her clients and their businesses into high gear, online & offline, and fast. Katrina is the creator of the JumpStart Your Marketing & Sales System, JumpStart Your Business System, and Jumpstart Yourself as a Speaker System. She is an 11x International Best-Selling Author with 20 books and CEO of Jumpstart Publishing as well. Katrina's first, hosted anthology book, *Jumpstart Your* ______ was published in Fall of 2018 and now every year Kat gets to help 12-20 entrepreneurs become authors as a new volume of *Jumpstart Your* _____ is published annually.

Katrina helps entrepreneurs make smarter marketing and business decisions in order to create the life and business of your dreams. She helps you create your big picture vision, plan and initial offerings if you're just starting out. She helps you develop a more leveraged, efficient business and marketing plan if you're more seasoned. Either way, she shows you all the steps, systems and marketing that need to be put in place in order to accomplish your big picture business, life and money goals. She does this via one-on-one coaching, her Live Big Mastermind, her Jumpstart Events, Webinars, Podcasts, and numerous Facebook groups she runs.

Katrina is the CEO of the International Speaker Network that meets twice monthly on Zoom for networking, resources and collaboration. She won the National Collaborator of the Year Award by the Public Speakers Association of who's conference which Katrina spoke for four years in a row. She is also a member of the Women's Speaker Association, eWomenNetwork, eWomen Speaker's Network, Women's Prosperity Network, and a Diamond Member of Polka Dot Powerhouse. Kat speaks to groups and conferences of all sizes all over North America and the Internet.

One thing that makes Katrina different is that she also focuses on her clients' personal lives. She found that most business owners lack enough self-confidence to truly enable them to get to their next level, or take those leaps of faith they need to achieve their ultimate dreams. This is the primary reason wrote her book, *Love Yourself Successful* back in 2012 and then released a 2nd Edition in 2022. Katrina's goal is to inspire, motivate, and educate entrepreneurs on how to love themselves fully, live a bigger life, and leverage themselves to complete happiness.

Katrina has a degree in Business Administration, Marketing Concentration, from California State University Sacramento, and has been a featured business expert on three of her local television news channels throughout her career thus far. She has also been featured in the Los Angeles Tribune, Comstock's Magazine, Lead Up for Women Magazine, Top Talent Magazine, and Amazing Women Magazine.

Katrina lives in Northern California with her husband Jason, and stepdaughter Riley, where she enjoys glamping in their 33-foot travel trailer, traveling, entertaining and of course, wine!

You can find out all about Kat and her products, programs, services, and live events online at

www.JumpstartYourBizNow.com,
www.JumpstartEvents.net,

www.JumpstartPublishing.net, and
www.iSpeakerNetwork.com.

Jumpstart
Resources

Motivate and Inspire Others!

“Share this Book”

Retail $16.95 + Tax & Shipping

Special Quantity Discounts

5 - 15 Books	$11.95 Each
16 - 30 Books	$9.95 Each
30 - 1,000 Books	$7.95 Each

To Place an Order Contact:

K. Sawa Marketing International Inc.
916-872-4000
info@JumpstartYourBizNow.com
or go to www.JumpstartPublishing.net

Grab One or More of the Jumpstart Your Business Free Trainings Now!

Learn How to:

- Get Started Speaking
- Jumpstart Your Business
- Implement Best Marketing Practices
- Build an Effective
- Website
- Create a Life You Love
- Find Your Purpose
- Love Yourself Successful
- Delegate & Build Your Team
- And more!

Get Access Online at:

www.JumpstartYourBizNow.com/ FreeTrainings

Want a Deeper Training on How to Start, Grow, Market & Monetize Your Business?

- In Depth Training, How-To, Templates
- Roadmap & Plan to Jumpstart Your Biz
- Hot Seat Coaching
- Learn from Topic Specific Speakers
- Mastermind & Network
- Make Money with Easy YES Offers

Attend One of Kat's Live Events!
Get Information at
www.JumpstartEvents.net

Book Katrina to Speak:

K. Sawa Marketing International Inc.
PO Box 6, Roseville, CA 95661
916-872-4000 |
info@JumpstartYourBizNow.com
www.JumpstartYourBizNow.com/speaking

Manufactured by Amazon.ca
Bolton, ON